ROUTLEDGE LIBRARY EDITIONS: PHILOSOPHY OF RELIGION

CHRISTIAN ETHICS

CHRISTIAN ETHICS

R. C. MORTIMER

Volume 25

LONDON AND NEW YORK

First published in 1950

This edition first published in 2013
by Routledge
2 Park Square, Milton Park, Abingdon, Oxon, OX14 4RN

Simultaneously published in the USA and Canada
by Routledge
711 Third Avenue, New York, NY 10017

Routledge is an imprint of the Taylor & Francis Group, an informa business

© 1950 R. C. Mortimer

All rights reserved. No part of this book may be reprinted or reproduced or utilised in any form or by any electronic, mechanical, or other means, now known or hereafter invented, including photocopying and recording, or in any information storage or retrieval system, without permission in writing from the publishers.

Trademark notice: Product or corporate names may be trademarks or registered trademarks, and are used only for identification and explanation without intent to infringe.

British Library Cataloguing in Publication Data
A catalogue record for this book is available from the British Library

ISBN: 978-0-415-65969-7 (Set)
eISBN: 978-0-203-52926-3 (Set)
ISBN: 978-0-415-82215-2 (Volume 25)
eISBN: 978-0-203-53459-5 (Volume 25)

Publisher's Note
The publisher has gone to great lengths to ensure the quality of this reprint but points out that some imperfections in the original copies may be apparent.

Disclaimer
The publisher has made every effort to trace copyright holders and would welcome correspondence from those they have been unable to trace.

 Printed and bound by CPI Group (UK) Ltd, Croydon, CR0 4YY

CHRISTIAN ETHICS

by

R. C. MORTIMER, D.D.

BISHOP OF EXETER, LATE
REGIUS PROFESSOR OF MORAL
AND PASTORAL THEOLOGY IN
THE UNIVERSITY OF OXFORD

1950
HUTCHINSON'S UNIVERSITY LIBRARY
Hutchinson House, London, W.1

New York   *Melbourne*   *Sydney*   *Cape Town*

THIS VOLUME IS NUMBER 49 IN
HUTCHINSON'S UNIVERSITY LIBRARY

*Printed in Great Britain by
Cheltenham Press Ltd.,
Cheltenham and London.*

CONTENTS

Chapter I	The Bible and Ethics	*Page*	7
II	Authority and Conscience		22
III	The Duty of Religion		42
IV	The Duty of Obedience		57
V	Social Duties		72
VI	Gambling		87
VII	Sex and Marriage		104
VIII	The Sanctity of Human Life		123
	Bibliography		139
	Index		141

CHAPTER I

THE BIBLE AND ETHICS

THE Christian religion is essentially a revelation of the nature of God. It tells men that God has done certain things. And from the nature of these actions we can infer what God is like. In the second place the Christian religion tells men what is the will of God for them, how they must live if they would please God. This second message is clearly dependent on the first. The kind of conduct which will please God depends on the kind of person God is. This is what is meant by saying that belief influences conduct. The once popular view that it does not matter what a man believes so long as he acts decently is nonsense. Because what he considers decent depends on what he believes. If you are a Nazi you will behave as a Nazi, if you are a Communist you will behave as a Communist, and if you are a Christian you will behave as a Christian. At least, in general. For a man does not always do what he knows he ought to do, and he does not always recognize clearly the implications for conduct of his belief. But in general our conduct, or at least our notions of what constitutes right conduct, are shaped by our beliefs. The man who knows about God—has a right faith—knows or may learn what conduct is pleasing to God and therefore right.

The Christian religion has a clear revelation of the nature of God, and by means of it instructs and enlightens the consciences of men. The first foundation is the doctrine of God the Creator. God made us and all the world. Because of that he has an absolute claim on our obedience. We do not exist in our own right, but only as His creatures, who ought therefore to do and be what He desires. We do not possess anything in the world, absolutely, not even our own bodies; we hold things in trust for God, who created them, and are bound, therefore, to use them only as He intends that they should be used. This is the doctrine contained in the first chapters of Genesis. God created man and placed him in the Garden of Eden with all the animals and the fruits of the earth at his disposal, subject to God's own law. "Of the fruit of the tree of the knowledge of good and evil thou shall not eat." Man's ownership and use of the material world is not absolute, but subject to the law of God.

From the doctrine of God as the Creator and source of all that is, it follows that a thing is not right simply because we think it is, still less because it seems to be expedient. It is right because God commands it. This means that there is a real distinction between right and wrong which is independent of what we happen to think. It is rooted in the nature and will of God. When a man's conscience tells him that a thing is right, which is in fact what God wills, his conscience is true and its judgement correct; when a man's conscience tells him a thing is right which is, in fact, contrary to God's will, his conscience is false and telling him a lie. It is a lamentably common experience for a man's conscience to play him false, so that in all good faith he does what is wrong, thinking it to be right. "Yea the time cometh that whosoever killeth you will think that he doeth God service." But this does not mean that whatever you think is right is right. It means that even conscience can be wrong: that the light which is in you can be darkness.

It is impossible to lay too great a stress on this fundamental principle, that there is a real and objective difference between right and wrong which is rooted in the will of God. It is the acceptance of this principle which distinguishes Christian ethics from Utilitarianism and Relativism. Utilitarianism distinguishes between right and wrong solely by reference to pleasure or expediency. That is right which tends to make me happy. The rightness of an action is to be judged by whether its consequences will bring more pleasure than pain, either to me or to society. By that, and that alone. When a man judges by reference to his own pleasure only, he is called a hedonist. Such a man is essentially selfish; for even though he may perform actions which give pleasure to others, his reason for doing so is that he himself derives pleasure from giving pleasure. That is why he thinks the action right. Utilitarians, properly so called, are those who think that right conduct consists not in pursuing their own pleasure but in promoting "the greatest happiness of the greatest number." In either case the decisive objection is that there is no means of distinguishing between one pleasure and another, except by its intensity. It is as right, perhaps more right, to indulge a passion for another man's wife than to listen to a classical concert. Moreover any action may be justified by its end : if, on balance, it causes more happiness than pain, it is right. Thus it would be right to murder an irritating mother-in-law and so restore peace and harmony to a whole family.

It is a curious irony that in the public mind Christian ethics have become identified with hedonistic utilitarianism. "Christian" conduct has come to mean kindness. And by kindness is meant giving people what they want. Thus it is unkind and "unchristian" to insist that married people should live together if they do not want to. It is unkind and "unchristian" to insist that a man should keep his word, when it has become irksome to do so. He would be so much happier if he broke his word, and we ought to promote happiness. The cause of this ironical situation lies in the partial truth contained in Utilitarianism. God does indeed desire men's happiness, and it is a duty to promote happiness and not to cause pain. But the human happiness which God desires is the happiness of maturity, of having reached our human goal of perfection. And for this many lower and transient pleasures have to be sacrificed, the good giving way to the better. The rightness of conduct has to be judged not in reference to the present only or to the immediate future—though these are relevant—but in reference also to the total good of the whole man, a good which extends beyond this life and is only fully realized in the society of heaven. Every man's true happiness lies in acquiring a full and developed personality, harmonious and controlled, and in taking his place in a community of such persons. Many of the things which we call happiness are, when persisted in, fatal obstacles to the growth of such a personality : many of the things which we call tragedies are its unavoidable birth-pangs. The distinction between right and wrong is the distinction between those things which foster and those which fatally hinder man's growth to perfect manhood, his attainment of his eternal destiny to be fully himself. What these things are which advance a man towards the true end of his nature, are determined, and immutably determined, by God the author of that nature. He has laid down the path of growth. Man cannot alter it. He can only fail to perceive it.

Relativism holds that there is no ultimate and objective distinction between right and wrong. It is all a matter of taste and opinion. Different people have different ideas. They are all equally right or equally wrong. Because there is not any real distinction. It is all a matter of how people feel about things. And that depends chiefly on how they were brought up. There are as many different codes as there are different societies and cultures. But these codes are only convenient patterns of behaviour. They do not correspond to anything in the nature of things, but either they are only devices on the part of those in power to keep their subjects docile, or else they are general, if unconscious, agreements between the individual members of a society for the sake of a quiet life. The logical conclusion from such a view is that superior and intelligent persons who see through this pretence are above the so-called moral law, and are free to do what they like. Their behaviour is not to be limited by any moral considerations but only by their power to get what they want. Might is right. The conclusion for less powerful and superior persons is that it is never any good arguing with people about right and wrong. People have different ideas. Live and let live. It is as stupid to be angry with a person who sees no wrong in being cruel to a child as it is to be angry with a person who likes eating snails. In the end this comes to a position of complete scepticism. Nobody *knows* anything about anything. They merely have ideas and opinions, likes and dislikes. It is improbable that anyone holds this view in its fulness, for we all have a strong bias towards believing and asserting that our own opinions are actually true and those of other people false. But it is this kind of relativism which underlies the modern tolerance of divergent codes of behaviour.

As against Utilitarianism and Relativism alike, Christianity holds strongly to the objective distinction between right and wrong. It appeals to the common-sense conviction that "I ought" does not mean the same thing as "I want" or "it would pay me." It appeals to the universal innate consent to the proposition that we must do good and avoid evil, and to the conviction that, in general and in outline, what is good and what is evil is the same for all men at all times, being determined by the intrinsic nature of man.

There is such a thing as human nature, which is the same in all men. It exists, like everything else, in order to become fully itself, to achieve its end. What that end is can be perceived, at any rate to a great extent, by the use of reason alone, unaided by any special divine revelation. For example, everybody has some idea of what is meant by a good man or a noble man. Everybody has some idea of what makes a society "advanced" or developed and what makes it primitive or decadent. Or again, that mind should control matter, the reason order the emotions, is clearly demanded by the very structure of our nature, in which there is a hierarchy of spirit, mind and body. To make the body obey the reason is in harmony with nature, to allow the body to dominate the mind is to violate nature. Temperance, self-control, has always been recognized as a virtue. Indeed there has always been a general recognition of what the virtues are : justice, courage, temperance, consideration for others. The man who has these is well on the way to realizing his true nature, to becoming a man. The coward, the thief, the libertine, the ruthless oppressor is stunting and maiming himself. He becomes less and less a man, as he becomes more and more the slave of some dominant impulse and obsession. He is unbalanced and only partially developed.

All this means that there is a pattern of general behaviour, a code of things to do and not to do, which derives necessarily from nature itself, from the simple fact that man is man. It is what is called natural law. The knowledge of it is not peculiar to Christians : it is common to man. It may make things plainer, to give an illustration or two.

It is clear that man's power of memory, by means of which he can use the experience of the past as a guide for the present and can in some measure forecast the future and so provide for coming needs out of present superfluity—it is clear that this power of memory indicates the duty of thrift and prudence and condemns prodigality as unnatural. Man is meant to acquire control of his environment by such use of reason and to live free of the bondage of chance and desperate need. Wilful neglect to make provision for the future is to violate the law of nature and to incur the risk of the penalties which such violations incur.

Again, nature makes it abundantly clear that the survival and education of human offspring require a long and close union of the two parents. Kittens and puppies may survive birth from promiscuous unions, being adequately cared for by the mother alone, and quickly reaching an age of self-sufficiency. Not so human babies, whose slow development to maturity involves them in a long helpless dependence on their parents, and creates for the parents a long period of shared responsibility for the lives they have brought into the world. Hence the institution of marriage, found at all levels of human culture, and the general recognition of the virtue of chastity and of fidelity to the marriage bond.

Again, it is clear that the isolated individual man, the fictional solitary inhabitant of a desert island, cannot, or does not easily attain to, the full development of his personality and power. It is by sharing the fruits of their diverse labour, by each contributing that for which he has a special aptitude, that men accumulate wealth, and by wealth get leisure. It is by mutual intercourse and the exchange of thought that men acquire and distribute wisdom, and are able to practise and appreciate the arts. It is by living together that men develop their spiritual and mental powers and become persons. In other words, as Aristotle said, Man is by nature a political animal. He is not meant to live alone but in society. From this follows the universal recognition of the virtue of justice. Without justice there can be no stable society.

Justice demands that all respect each other's rights, so that all may live together in peaceable enjoyment of that which is their own. The particular determinations of justice, the decision as to what are each man's rights has always been difficult, and subject to constant variation; but the general principle that rights are to be respected has been universally admitted and finds expression in such universal prohibitions as "thou shalt not kill" and "thou shalt not steal."

The fact that there is (in this way) a pattern of behaviour by which alone man can attain to his full stature, that this pattern is laid down by the constitution of his nature as created by God, and that it can, at least in part and in general, be perceived by the light of unaided reason, that it can indeed be so easily perceived that in many cases it appears to be self-evident and axiomatic, so that ignorance of it is impossible to all but infants and imbeciles—for who can be ignorant that adultery is wrong or truthfulness right. All this must not be allowed to involve us in the error of supposing that this pattern of behaviour or natural law is a ready-made code, which every man has only to look within himself to read. The application of this law to the changing circumstances of evolving societies leaves room for every sort of error. And our knowledge of it is still crude and capable of endless refinement, as we penetrate more deeply into the mystery which surrounds human nature and sharpen our moral sensitiveness.

It is certain that human perception of the content and implications of natural law has developed with the emergence of man from his primitive condition—the history of the institution of marriage is but one, if the clearest, illustration of this. It is equally certain that it has also regressed; that from time to time different human societies have lost, or failed to reach, a grasp of certain of the most elementary of its contents. Anthropologists have little difficulty in showing that there is scarcely one of the generally accepted moral axioms which has not somewhere at some time been denied. Cannibalism, thievery, even prostitution have in some societies not merely been practised, but extolled as moral duties. And in our own day we have been amazed at the

Nazi moral code, which inculcated cruelty and lies as patriotic virtues.

Some have used these facts as an argument in favour of relativism and against the very existence of a natural law of divinely constituted human behaviour. But the facts will not bear this argument, any more than ignorance of the solar system proves that the earth does not go round the sun. Existence of law and knowledge of that law are not the same thing. The law may well exist, and yet men be in ignorance of it. Knowledge of the law of nature in its more delicate implications and determinations demands refinement of moral sensitiveness and a quality of prophetic insight. Even in its elementary content, in such precepts as the ten commandments, passion, self-interest, long-standing custom can blind men to truths which to others seem self-evident. The elementary right to individual freedom has often been denied to slaves in the name of the law of nature itself. There is no limit to the perversity of the human reason when clouded and weakened by unredeemed sin. It is the fact of universal human selfishness, or as theologians call it, the Fall, which prevents men from attaining a clear and persistent understanding of what constitutes right behaviour. And it is this which establishes the permanent need of Revelation, and places Christians in a privileged and especially responsible position.

The pattern of conduct which God has laid down for man is the same for all men. It is universally valid. When we speak of Christian ethics we do not mean that there is one law for Christians and another for non-Christians. We mean the Christian understanding and statement of the one common law for all men. Unbelievers also know or can be persuaded of that law or of part of it: Christians have a fuller and better knowledge. The reason for this is that Christians have by revelation a fuller and truer knowledge both of the nature of God Himself and of the nature of man. As has been well said, "Christian men, in order to learn what is the place of the Natural Law and its products in the economy of salvation, must look to the Bible as the witness of God's operations and as the record of God's supernatural destiny for man, to which the Natural Law is itself orientated and subordinated. Only with such a perspective, and with the will to purification of perception and purpose thereby created, will they be able to perceive or affirm the Natural Law in its completeness as an expression of the Lordship of Jesus Christ." (*Natural Law*. Edited by A. M. Vidler and W. A. Whitehouse. S.C.M. Press 1945. Page 24.)

The Revelation in the Bible plays a three-fold part. In the first place it recalls and restates in simple and even violent language fundamental moral judgements which men are always in danger of forgetting or explaining away. It thus provides a norm and standard of human behaviour in the broadest and simplest outline. Man's duty to worship God and love the truth, to respect lawful authority, to refrain from violence and robbery, to live in chastity, to be fair and even merciful in his dealings with his neighbour—and all this as the declared will of God, the way man *must* live if he would achieve his end—this is the constant theme of the Bible. The effect of it is not to reveal something new which men could not have found out for themselves, but to recall them to what they have forgotten or with culpable blindness have failed to perceive.

It is not easy to exaggerate the power of human self-deception nor man's ingenuity in persuading himself that black is white; manifest injustice can be depicted as justice, and unchastity acclaimed as "a venture of bold living." For example in times of shortages to exploit the needs and miseries of the poor by a strictly legal use of the markets may easily be represented as a perfectly proper use of one's opportunities, a quite legitimate advancement of oneself and one's family. The complacency born of such long and widespread practice is shattered by the violence of Revelation. "Thus saith the Lord: For three transgressions of Israel, and for four, I will not turn away the punishment thereof; because they sold the righteous for silver and the poor for a pair of shoes. . . ." (Amos ii, 6). This, then, is the first work of Revelation; it continuously sets forth the broad paths of right conduct. Lies are lies by whatever name you call them, and injustice is injustice however fairly screened and decked. They who read the Scriptures constantly and with attention cannot fail to ask themselves not only how far they have knowingly and wilfully transgressed the law of God, but also how far even that conduct which has seemed above question and reproach comes under divine condemnation.

And this leads to the second work of Revelation. The conduct which God demands of men, He demands out of His own Holiness and Righteousness. "Be ye perfect, as your Father in Heaven is perfect." Not the service of the lips but of the heart, not obedience in the letter but in the Spirit is commanded. The standard is too high: the Judge too all-seeing and just. The grandeur and majesty of the moral law proclaims the weakness and impotence of man. It shatters human pride and self-sufficiency: it overthrows that complacency with which the righteous regard the tattered robes of their partial virtues, and that satisfaction with which rogues rejoice to discover other men more evil than themselves. The revelation of the holiness of God and His Law, once struck home, drives men to confess their need of grace and brings them to Christ their Saviour.

Lastly, revelation, by the light which it throws on the nature of God and man, suggests new emphases and new precepts, a new scale of values which could not at all, or could not easily, have been perceived as part of the Natural Law for man without it. Thus it comes about that Christian ethics is at once old and new. It covers the same ground of human conduct as the law of the Old Testament and the "law of the Gentiles written in their hearts." Many of its precepts are the same precepts. Yet all is seen in a different light and in a new perspective—the perspective of God's love manifested in Christ. It will be worth while to give one or two illustrations of this.

Revelation throws into sharp relief the supreme value of each individual human being. Every man is an immortal soul created by God and designed for an eternal inheritance. The love of God effected by the Incarnation the restoration and renewal of fallen human nature in order that all men alike might benefit thereby. The Son of God showed particular care and concern for the fallen, the outcast, the weak and the despised. He came, not to call the righteous, but sinners to repentance. Like a good shepherd, He sought especially for the sheep which was lost. Moreover, the divine drama of Calvary which was the cost of man's redemption, the price necessary to give him again a clear picture of what human nature was designed to be and to provide him with the inspiration to strive towards it and the assurance that he is not irrevocably tied and bound to his sinful, selfish past, makes it equally clear that in the eyes of the Creator His creature man is of infinite worth and value.

The lesson is plain and clear : all men equally are the children of God, all men equally are the object of His love. In consequence of this, Christian ethics has always asserted that every man is a person possessed of certain inalienable rights, that he is an end in himself never to be used merely as a means to something else. And he is this in virtue of his being a man, no matter what his race or colour, no matter how well or poorly endowed with talents, no matter how primitive or developed. And further, since man is an end in himself, and that end transcends this world of time and space, being fully attained only in heaven, it follows that the individual takes precedence over society, in the sense that society exists for the good of its individual members, not those members for society. However much the good of the whole is greater than the good of any one of its parts, and whatever the duties each man owes to society, individual persons constitute the supreme value, and society itself exists only to promote the good of those persons.

This principle of the infinite worth of the individual is explicit in Scripture, and in the light of it all totalitarian doctrines of the State stand condemned. However, the implications of this principle for human living and for the organization of society are not explicit, but need to be perceived and worked out by the human conscience. How obtuse that conscience can be, even when illumined by revelation, is startlingly illustrated by the long centuries in which Christianity tolerated the institution of slavery. In view of the constant tendency of man to exploit his fellow men and use them as the instruments of his greed and selfishness, two things are certain. First, that the Scriptural revelation of the innate inalienable dignity and value of the individual is an indispensable bulwark of human freedom and growth. And second, that our knowledge of the implication of this revelation is far indeed from being perfect; there is constant need of further refinement of our moral perceptions, a refinement which can only emerge as the fruit of a deeper penetration of the Gospel of God's love into human life and thought.

Another illustration of the effect of Scripture upon ethics is given by the surrender of the principle of exact retribution in favour of the principle of mercy. Natural justice would seem to require exact retributive punishment, an eye for an eye, a tooth for a tooth. The codes of primitive peoples, and the long history of blood feuds show how the human conscience has approved of this concept. The revelation of the divine love and the explicit teaching of the Son of God have demonstrated the superiority of mercy, and have pointed the proper rôle of punishment as correction and not vengeance. Because of the revelation that in God justice is never unaccompanied by mercy, in Christian ethics there has always been an emphasis on the patient endurance of wrongs in imitation of Calvary, and on the suppression of all emotions of vindictive anger. As a means to soften human relations, as a restraint of human anger and cruelty, so easily disguised under the cloak of justice, the history of the world has nothing to show comparable to this Christian emphasis on patience and mercy, this insistence that even the just satisfaction of our wrongs yields to the divine example of forbearance. We are to be content with the reform or at least the restraint of the evil-doer, never to seek or demand vengeance.

It is well known how great a store Aristotle set by the "magnanimous" man, the man who holds himself to be intellectually and morally superior to his fellows, and is so. The concept of humility as a virtue is, I think, peculiar to the Christian code of ethics. It is inspired wholly by the example of the Son of God who came down from heaven and lived as man, and suffered the shameful death of the

Cross. "The Son of Man came not to be ministered unto but to minister." "He that is greatest among you, let him be as one that serveth."

The duty of the great and highly placed not to seek their own advantage, but to devote themselves to the service of those over whom they bear rule: the conviction that all are equal in the sight of God, though different men have different functions: the recognition that all authority, power and wealth are from above, held in trust for God to whom account must one day be given: the understanding that respect, deference, prestige, rank are not things to be eagerly grasped at, but that, in imitation of Him who counted not His equality with God a prize to be snatched at, their surrender is nobler than their acquisition, their responsibility weightier than their privileges: these are insights not easily gained by the natural man, but plain in the Revelation and always emphasized in the Christian tradition. Humility in high and low alike is that virtue by which men are conscious of their own frailty and unworthiness, and grateful for the divine mercy and help upon which they constantly depend; by it they see in their own virtues only the triumph of God's grace and a divine commission to the service of others. This lovely quality is perhaps the noblest of all the gifts of Christianity to the human race.

Closely allied to humility is courtesy. Genuine good manners as distinct from conventional behaviour spring from consideration for others, and presuppose a readiness to sacrifice our own convenience and comfort together with a spontaneous concession of the equal dignity or greater need of others. They are the direct opposite of selfish and insensitive greed. They cover the whole range of human behaviour, have their place in every situation and are due to men of every rank and age and class. They are not capable of compressed definition: they are summed up in the behaviour of a Christian gentleman. They are rooted in the divine example of self-sacrifice and in the revelation of the divine care for the weak, outcast and wretched. They are shown in the Christian tradition of giving place to others, of offering assistance to the weak, of sympathy and respect for physical deformity, of endeavouring to alleviate pain and tend sickness. They cannot be taught or practised apart from the content of the divine command to love our neighbour and the divine example of the Son of Man. They become the instinctive and spontaneous behaviour of those to whom the Gospels are familiar and loved reading.

A last and familiar example of the corrective influence of Revelation upon the sin-darkened conscience of the human race is provided by the enhanced status of women in the Christian tradition. The certainty that women share equally with men in human nature and are therefore also of infinite value and worth, is implicit in the revelation which sternly forbids the use of them as mere instruments of male lust. Their physical weakness relative to men arouses the Christian impulse to defend and care for the weak. The conviction that though all have not the same office yet all are members of the one Body, all are equally the children of God, corrects the natural tendency to male superiority and prevents any permanent relegation of women to an inferior position. There is diversity of function, but essentially and in all that matters most equality of status. Above all, the taking by the Godhead of human flesh within the womb of our Lady has sanctified all motherhood and powerfully reinforced the natural human instinct of reverence for feminine chastity.

These are only a few of the matters on which the human conscience is enlightened by the revelation contained in the Christian tradition. Nor are all the implications of the Revelation anything like fully realized even now after nearly two thousand years. No doubt so long as humanity exists, among those who humbly and patiently seek to live under the Gospel there will develop an ever clearer and more delicate perception of what the divine pattern for human conduct is. It is certain that where the Revelation is ignored, the darkness of degeneracy and barbarism sets in. Sin-ridden man needs the Scriptures to rebuke his errors, to correct the distortion with which he perceives the natural law, to hold him firmly to its elementary principles and to lighten his eyes to its hidden depths. Christian ethics is the exposition of the moral truths implicit in the Revelation, and the application of them to human living. It interprets to man the natural law on the basis of that superior knowledge of the nature of God, of man and of the end for which man is created, which Revelation contains.

CHAPTER II

AUTHORITY AND CONSCIENCE

BECAUSE the content of Christian ethics is thus determined by the nature of the divine revelation in Scripture, the Church has always held a high position of authority in the matter of morals. Just as it is her duty and function to define what is the Christian faith, and to guard it from false teaching, so it is her duty to define what is the Christian conduct which follows from that faith, and to denounce practices which are opposed to it. The most important part of her duty in this respect is to proclaim the broad principles and general duties of Christian behaviour. It is her duty constantly to remind men of those obvious moral truths which they are always in danger of forgetting under the influence of passion and self-interest. The "duty towards God" and "the duty towards my neighbour" in the English Church Catechism are illustrations of the Church performing this kind of work. The two "duties" set out the ordinary Christian duties. They are stated without argument and on authority—the authority of Scripture and of the Church interpreting Scripture. The clergy, armed with the same authority, preach these duties and expound them.

In addition to this duty of constantly emphasizing general principles, the Church has also the duty of applying these principles to changing circumstances. This is a task of very considerable difficulty—a difficulty not clearly realized by those who glibly call "for a lead from the Church" whenever any fresh moral problem arises. The difficulty is created by the tension between the "magisterium" or "teaching authority" of the Church in faith and morals on the one hand, and the autonomy of every individual conscience on the other.

Once the Church has "pronounced" on any question of

morals, there is a prima facie obligation on Christians to obey: for the Church has authority in such matters. Yet if the pronouncement is contrary to a man's own conscientious judgement there is a higher obligation, as we shall see in a moment, to obey one's own conscience. It is for this reason, in order to avoid a conflict of this kind, that the Protestant Churches, at least, are reluctant to issue detailed and authoritative statements on new moral problems. After all, the guidance of the Holy Spirit is promised to the Church as a whole, the Spirit dwells in every member of the Church from the highest and most instructed to the lowest and least gifted. Authoritative pronouncements are only properly made when they express and articulate the common mind of the whole Church. To determine what this mind is is a slow and difficult matter. It is not necessarily what those in authority in the Church hold to be true at the moment of the first impact of the new problem; neither is it necessarily the half-instinctive reaction of the general mass of Christians. The common Spirit-guided judgement more often emerges or crystallises slowly after debate and reflection.

Nevertheless, life has to be lived. And men naturally and rightly demand of the Church help and advice in solving their moral problems and in applying the principles of Christian ethics to the situations in which they daily find themselves. It is much easier to perceive and admit, for example, the claims of justice in general, than to decide what is in fact just within the framework of a given social order. The Church has an undeniable duty to ease this difficulty, sometimes by re-proclaiming the general principles and outline of justice, sometimes by going further and asserting positively that this or that practice is demanded or is condemned by those principles. This duty brings the Church not only into the area of personal ethics but also into the spheres of politics and economics. Her voice is to be heard both declaring and expounding, for example, the duties of marriage and also teaching the laws of war, the requirements of honesty in business or the mutual duties of employer and employed.

In many cases, perhaps in most, the Church does not try

so much to lay down the solutions of moral problems or to dictate in detail the moral conduct appropriate to particular circumstances, as to set forth the principles which must be borne in mind by those faced with such problems, and with which conduct must conform in this or that set of circumstances. Thus, in time of war, the Church will not necessarily condemn out of hand any particular method of warfare—for she may have altogether inadequate material for passing a judgement—but she will remind belligerents of the duties of mercy and humanity and of the general claims of justice. And in this way she will call on those in authority to see to it that their conduct of the war does not infringe these principles. Or again, in matters of the market place, the Church will not herself lay down what is the just price, or at what point profits turn into profiteering: she will not herself determine what is a fair wage, or what is the proper number of hours to be worked in a day or a week. But she will insist that merchants aim at a just price, that manufacturers be content with a moderate profit, that masters and men have a common Master in Heaven, that the labourer is worthy of his hire, that power and advantage are not rightly used as opportunities to exploit or coerce. And she will call on all those engaged in the market place to see to it that in their conduct they do not wilfully and flagrantly violate those principles.

When new inventions suddenly create new situations, it becomes the duty of the Church to assist Christians to form their moral judgements by stating clearly the moral issues which are involved. She assists them by showing what is genuinely new in the new situation and what is old, by disentangling the various elements which go to form the situation, and so presenting a clearer picture of the problem which has to be solved.

These are some of the ways in which the Protestant Churches, at least, try to discharge their duty of guiding and teaching Christian people in matters of morals. Occasionally, and in the case of the Roman Church more often, the Church will authoritatively forbid particular practices as certainly contrary to the laws of God. For example, divorce and re-marriage is condemned as a violation of the marriage-bond. The compulsory sterilisation of the mentally defective is forbidden as constituting a denial of an essential human right, and their extermination as an unjustifiable subordination of the individual to the community. The institution of slavery is condemned as unjust in its affront to human dignity and its denial of human rights.

Whether the Church commands or reminds or advises, precisely because she is the divinely constituted guardian and interpreter of the Christian faith in which Christian ethics is rooted, her voice is not to be disregarded. She is not to be carelessly and lightly dismissed as though she had no right to speak, and were guilty of an unwarrantable intrusion into matters outside the sphere of religion. All Christians are morally bound to pay her the greatest attention; they are to take account in their conduct of those principles which she lays down as governing particular matters, and where she issues a definite command or prohibition, they are under a moral obligation to obey. Yet, because the application of moral principles to particular situations and the consequent determination of where duty lies is the primary task of the individual conscience, the Church, however authoritative her teaching, is not the final arbiter. The last word lies with conscience.

The statement that Christians are under a moral obligation to obey the Church in matters of morals presupposes that their own consciences are not at variance with the teaching of the Church. No man may lightly set up his own judgement against that of the Church, nor acquiesce in conscientious disagreement without the most serious and painful effort to understand and make his own the Church's judgement; but in the last resort his own conscience must be allowed to be supreme. Deeply embedded in the heart of Christian ethics is the dictum "Conscience is always to be obeyed."

It must be so. Conscience is a man's reason making moral judgements. It is by the use of his reason that man apprehends truth, if he apprehends it at all. What, therefore, a man perceives to be true he must hold to be true or else deny that he can ever perceive truth at all.

A judgement of conscience is a perception or apprehension of moral truth. It takes the form "this is right" or "this is wrong." The foundation of all morality is the innate instinctive universal recognition that right is to be done, wrong is not to be done. When, therefore, a man judges, by his reason, that "this is right," at the same moment he recognizes that "this ought to be done." To hold that "this is right, yet it ought not to be done" is the same as to say "this is right, though I know it to be wrong" or "I accept as true what I know to be untrue." In other words a man can never be acting rightly when he goes against his conscience.

This does not mean, as we shall see in a moment, that he is necessarily acting rightly whenever he obeys his conscience. It is nonsense to suppose that whatever a man thinks is right must be right. But it does mean that whenever a man disobeys his conscience, whether his conscience is right or wrong, he is acting wrongly. For every time he does so, he says in effect "I am doing what I judge to be wrong." Hence, in the last resort, no matter how much others may denounce my judgement as false, no matter with what authority of tradition and learning the contrary opinion be invested, if my own conscience is clear and certain it must be followed. For not to follow it would be to refuse to do what I know to be right, what I know to be the will of God.

From this fundamental principle of the supremacy of the individual conscience, as constituting for each individual the norm and standard of moral conduct from which there is no appeal, there flow two important corollaries. The first is that it becomes at times a duty to disobey lawful authority. The second is that it is at all times a duty to take moral problems seriously.

Although, as we shall see, it is the teaching of Christian ethics that subjects are under a moral obligation to obey their lawful superiors—that such obedience is the will of God, to be rendered "for conscience sake" and not merely from compulsion—yet the obedience so enjoined is not blind and undiscriminating. It is due to superiors because and in so far as they are the agents of God. It follows, therefore, that no obedience is due where the superiors command anything which is against the will of God. On the contrary, such commands not only may but must be disobeyed. For we are to obey God rather than men. In consequence it is the duty of subjects in every state to scrutinise the laws passed upon them, to make sure that they will not, by obeying them, transgress the laws of God. In a democratic state they have the further duty of taking the appropriate constitutional steps to have such laws repealed and to ensure that no more such laws be enacted.

Two practical illustrations of this occasional duty of the subject to disobey the law may be given. The first is that of the conscientious objector. If a man is convinced that war is essentially sinful, that in no circumstances whatsoever is it ever right to engage in war, then he is in conscience bound to refuse to take any part in war. If the law orders him to join the armed forces, or to make munitions or to do anything which directly and exclusively furthers the prosecution of a war, he is bound to refuse. Even if the consequences are imprisonment or death as a traitor, he is bound to refuse. For he must obey his own conscience—that is the command of God as he understands it—rather than men. It is evidence of the impact of Christianity upon our society that in England this duty to obey conscience is recognized, and obedience to law is not enforced when it is known to meet with conscientious objection. Even though a door be opened to abuse, and cowardly evasion be given an opportunity of masquerading as conscientious conviction, still it is held to be better for the community and more in accordance with true morality that some, perhaps many, be allowed "to get away with it" rather than that anyone should be compelled or driven by threats to deny his conscience. The rights of conscience, the right of a man to be allowed to do his duty as he sees it, are supreme.

The second illustration is that of a clergyman who under "the seal of confession" has learnt the identity of a criminal and so possesses convincing evidence of the criminal's guilt. It is a "moral impossibility" for a clergyman to reveal to others what he has been told as part of a "confession." He knows that the Sacrament of Penance has been instituted by God for the restoration and comfort of sinners. He knows that what he is told, he is told not as a fellow-man or fellow-citizen, but as a priest and representative of God. He knows that men make use of the confessional in the unquestioned certainty that whatever is said there is never by word or deed, by hint or innuendo, passed on. He knows that he is the inheritor and guardian of an honourable tradition which he must not, dare not, break. If he were forced into the witness-box, and threatened with the direst penalties of the law if he did not reveal all that he knew, he would be bound to refuse, be the consequences what they may.

The same would perhaps be true of a doctor who received information from a patient on the understanding, explicit or even implicit, that there exists a code of professional conduct which forbids the publication of any knowledge so acquired. For the doctor would necessarily hold himself bound in conscience to respect the confidence which had been placed in him, because the confidence was given to him not as an individual, but as a doctor, and was given on the understanding that in *no* circumstances would it be betrayed.

It is said among lawyers to be a matter of doubt whether the law which requires every citizen to give full and truthful evidence when called upon to do so in a court of law, is enforceable against a priest, or even against a doctor. There are grounds for holding that the priest in respect of what he learns by hearing confessions and the doctor in respect of "professional secrets" are privileged in the same way that a wife is privileged and excused from the necessity of giving evidence against her husband. In the interests of Christian morality it is much to be hoped that this is so. And this not only because it is for the good both of individuals and of the community that persons in moral and mental difficulty or anguish should be encouraged to unburden their griefs by the certainty that in so doing they will not jeopardise their own security and reputation, but much more because these cases are acute instances of the duty of conscientious disobedience to the general law. Priests and doctors so situated "can do no other." To invoke the machinery and penalties of the law in an effort to force them to go against their consciences is barbaric and unchristian. Yet, whatever the state of the law in England on this point may be, the duty of the individuals concerned is clear. If the penalties of the law can be invoked against them, they must submit to those penalties, but continue to refuse their evidence. Their own conscience is supreme.

It is happily true that in England it is not easy to imagine the circumstances in which the law would command actions which the individual could not conscientiously perform. The laws of England are based in general on morality as understood and taught in the Christian tradition. And that Christian tradition is still so influential that few acts are likely to find their way on to the Statute Book which are recognized as being contrary to Christian morality, and any act imposing obligations to which there are known to be conscientious objections on the part of a minority will almost certainly contain provisions for the non-compliance of that minority. Respect for the individual conscience is not the least of the gifts which democracy, as we understand it, owes to the Christian religion. And the chiefest safeguard against, and obstacle to, autocratic totalitarian governments is provided by this same Christian religion with its insistence on the overriding duty for every man to obey his own conscience, no matter what the consequences may be.

This insistence on the rights of conscience has its counterpart in Christian ethics in the insistence on the duty of every man to take moral problems seriously. There is no protection afforded for mere prejudice and bigotry, still less for whims and fancies. If government is required to respect the individual's conscience, the individual is likewise required to make every effort to arrive at a true and informed judgement. This requirement follows necessarily from the principle that conscience is for each man the norm and standard of conduct. Thus every man has an obligation not only to obey his conscience in all things, but also to do all that he reasonably can to ensure that his conscience is true and not false, so that the conduct which it commands is, in fact, right conduct. In other words, he must take moral problems seriously.

The first rule is to obey conscience. Where conscience gives a clear ruling, deliberately and knowingly to disobey it is sinful. The concept of sin plays a large part in Christian ethics. Its form and essence is deliberate disobedience to God. It is the work of conscience to tell a man on every occasion what is the will of God. Hence, to disobey conscience is to disobey God. It often happens, of course, that what a man's conscience tells him to do is not in fact God's will. Yet even so, to disobey conscience is to disobey God; for the man refuses to do what he *thinks* is God's will. If a father tells his child not to walk on the beds, and the child takes that to refer to his bedroom and not to the garden, the child is clearly a disobedient child if he walks on his bed in his bedroom. If he walks on the beds in the garden, though he does what his father does not want him to do, he is not, because of his misunderstanding, committing an act of disobedience. From this it would seem to follow that a man is never guilty of sin so long as he obeys his conscience. Yet this is an over-simplification. Obedience to conscience does not always excuse from sin.

This is because sometimes a man is himself responsible for his conscience being wrong. In such a case the sin lies not so much in the disobedience as in "the not knowing better." Yet this "not knowing better" is a form of disobedience. For not to trouble to find out God's will when we can argues an indifference as to what God's will is: and such an indifference means that we do not care whether we do God's will or not; and this is the essential spirit of disobedience. The child who hears his father say "Do not walk on the beds" and thinks his father said "do not walk on the bed" may be guilty of culpable inattention. He really was not listening to what his father said. But not to listen is proof of indifference and so of a disobedient spirit. He may indeed be guilty of something worse—of deliberate misunderstanding. He may be so anxious to walk on the beds that he will not allow himself to consider whether it is really likely that his father said "do not walk on the bed," whether it is not in fact much more probable that he was referring to the garden beds. By a deliberate act of will he contrives to prevent his conscience from telling him "you ought not to walk on the garden beds."

We all have a duty to do what in us lies to see that our conscience is rightly informed. If we neglect this duty, and it is our fault that our conscience is wrongly informed, then the action dictated by the wrong conscience is laid at our door, and is sinful. We ought to have known better. That is what is meant by the duty to take moral problems seriously. We are guilty if we arrive at a wrong moral decision carelessly and lightheartedly, because we are not willing to take reasonable trouble, or because we suspect that a little scrutiny might well involve us in a decision which we do not want. If it is certainly a sin to do what our conscience tells us is clearly wrong, it is also a sin to allow the conscience to become blunt or to rest in ignorance. It will be worth while to add a practical illustration of all this.

Let us suppose that I have just obtained employment in a furniture factory. I find that it is a universal custom for any employee who likes to take home with him some of the wood on which he works, and to make out of it toys for his children, or to sell. At first I fall in with this custom with delight and think nothing of it. I assume that it has the approval of the employers, and that it is one of the employees' recognized perquisites. After a while I begin to doubt. Do the employers really approve ? Do they even know that it is going on ? Or if they do, do they tolerate it only because they are powerless to stop it ? And if that is the case, is not the practice really stealing ? It is possible for me to stifle this doubt, by refusing to think any more about it. That is to refuse to take a moral problem seriously. I am content to take things as they are and not to raise difficulties. "Oh, I don't know. I expect it's all right." This is simple sinful negligence.

Now suppose that while I am in this condition, one of my fellow-workers consults me on this very matter. "Do I think it is all right?" This necessarily re-awakens and reinforces my doubt. I can no longer simply ignore it, as I have been able to do so far. But what I can do is to set it aside deliberately, and resolve to go on taking the wood, as though I was certain it was all right. "Ask no questions and you'll be told no lies." I do not *know* that it is stealing, so I shall assume that it is not. It would be very unwise to ask any questions, because it might turn out to be quite clearly stealing. It is obvious that by pursuing such a course I am myself responsible for the erring condition of my conscience. It is perfectly possible for me to say truthfully if found out, "I did not know that it was stealing. I thought it was all right." But I am personally responsible for my ignorance, which is wilful and deliberate.

No doubt, so far I have taken the easiest course. I have been content in spite of doubts to rely on the assumption that what everybody does must be permissible, and I have been able to set my conscience at rest in that way. What I ought to have done was to make further enquiries. Of course the simplest way to solve my difficulties is to ask my employers, but this may not be feasible. In that case, I can ask first some of my fellow-employees, then a foreman and then a manager. I may, even so, get conflicting answers. The employees and the foreman may honestly think that the wood is a legitimate perquisite: the manager may consider it his duty to protect the employer's property and feel himself unable to authorize the practice, consequently he is bound to say that the practice is wrong. I may now consult someone outside whose judgement I respect and who can give a wholly impartial answer. He may tell me that in his view the employer's consent may reasonably be presumed. First, because on the general principle that "thou shalt not muzzle the ox that treadeth out the corn" it is proper that the workmen should be allowed a small amount of wood for their own purposes. Secondly, because the practice must be well-known to the employers, who, if they disapproved of it would put up notices forbidding it. The absence of such notices must be taken to imply that they prefer to allow the practice to go on. Thirdly, in many factories, e.g. tobacco and sweet factories, the employees are allowed a specified quantity of the factory products for nothing, or at cost price. The employers could make a similar regulation here if they wished. Since they have not forbidden the practice altogether, nor made such a regulation, it may be presumed that they prefer to trust their employees to take only so much wood as is reasonable. What is reasonable may be inferred in part from a comparison of other factories where there are such regulations, and in part by considering that it is unreasonable to suppose that the employers intend wood to be taken which is easily capable of being used in the factory for the articles which they customarily manufacture. That is to say it is only discarded or unsuitable wood which may properly be taken.

This answer may be right or may be wrong. But if I am convinced by it that the practice which worried me is a legitimate one, I cannot be blamed for moral laxity in acting upon it. I have taken such reasonable steps as are possible to find out the rights and wrongs of the matter, and even though I have arrived at a wrong conclusion, at least I have taken the matter seriously, and am not to blame for my conscience being in error.

Often, indeed, it happens that we are not to blame for our conscience being in error, even when we have made no enquiry at all. This is because a man cannot doubt what he apprehends as certain; and if he does not doubt, he cannot enquire. If we have lived all our lives in an environment where some action has always been thought right by everybody and no question about it has ever been raised, it is likely that we shall assume it to be right without any doubt ever crossing our minds. A member of a cannibalistic tribe will think cannibalism lawful, and unless its wrongness is suggested to him by somebody, or a doubt arises in his mind of its own accord, he is not to blame if he never raises the question but eats human flesh with an untroubled conscience. Modern methods of propaganda have much the same effect. It is possible so to condition people's minds that they will accept certain ethical propositions as indubitably true, having been made psychologically incapable of doubting them.

When people have been long exposed to slogans which are enthusiastically believed by all around them, they cannot be blamed if they also come to accept the truth of those slogans uncritically and blindly. The development of the technique of propaganda has caused a serious restriction of the area in which free conscientious judgement is possible. There are many things which men do which seem to an unbiased and "unconditioned" outsider to be patently and flagrantly immoral, but the morality of which seems above question to those who do them. For example, there are many so-called "restrictive practices" in the industrial world which appear to the outsider to be obviously unjust in that they deprive the employer of a fair return of labour for the wages which he pays. But to the employee the matter presents itself quite differently. He has been nourished in the fear of unemployment; he has been brought up in an atmosphere of suspicion towards all employers; he has been constantly told that he has in the past been and is now unfairly exploited; he is exhorted to show loyalty to his weaker brethren by accommodating his strength and skill to their weakness and clumsiness. So "conditioned," restrictive practices seem to him self-evidently just and loyal.

In the face of "conditioning" and propaganda it is necessary to use great caution in applying the axiom that it is a duty always to take moral problems seriously. All men are not always to blame when they brush aside contemptuously doubts and suggestions which appear to an outsider to be unquestionably grave and disturbing. Nevertheless the axiom can and should be ruthlessly applied whenever a doubt is perceived to be solid and well-grounded. In such cases there is no excuse for ignoring the doubt and resting content in the old unquestioning position.

A serious doubt may arise in many ways. The apparent injustice of a hitherto unquestioned practice may suddenly be perceived or suggested by a reading of the Bible. In such a case enquiry must be made as to whether it is in fact unjust or not. Or the doubt may come because of an open denunciation of the practice by others whose opinion rightly commands respectful consideration, for example, by the

Church or by the Government. Or the doubt may arise when conduct so far unquestioned is found to lead to conduct which has hitherto been condemned. For example, a man brought up and "conditioned" to hold that loyalty and obedience to a party are the supreme principles of conduct to which all else must be subordinated, can scarcely fail to doubt the truth of this position when he is required by those principles to perform an action which hitherto he has always regarded as wrong. If he is ordered to carry out a work of sabotage which must involve the deaths of innocent persons, or if he is commanded to lie and to cheat those who have been his friends, he cannot fail to doubt whether such actions can really be right and whether loyalty is the supreme principle of conduct. And so doubting, he cannot be held free from blame if he performs them without further enquiry.

The rule is that wherever there is serious doubt and uneasiness there must be enquiry. There must be a genuine effort to arrive at objective truth. No man is excused for doing what he knows to be wrong, or suspects may be wrong, simply because a great many other people do it and see no harm in it. If he thinks it may be wrong, it is his duty to stop and enquire. The amount of care and thought which should be given to any moral problem depends on the importance of the matter involved. We are not to spend our lives worrying over trifles. The test and standard is what is reasonable in the circumstances—have we done what any reasonable and prudent man would do, to make sure that our conduct is right ?

A prudent man in a state of doubt and uncertainty will do three things. First, he will pray to God for wisdom and enlightenment: he will pray for protection against selfish bias, against being blinded by passion or self-interest. Such prayers are never unanswered. Secondly, he will use his own reason, to try and see for himself where the truth lies. Thirdly, he will betake himself to books, especially the Bible, and will ask the advice of more experienced persons than himself, whose wisdom and goodness he has cause to respect; and he will listen to and ponder what they have to say. When he has done all this in a sincere attempt to resolve his doubt, he will have done all that a reasonable and prudent man can do to inform his conscience. Whatever he decides will be a conscientious decision, and its wrongness—if it is wrong—will not be imputable to him.

Thus Christian ethics puts in the forefront the supremacy of conscience and the duty of keeping one's conscience alert and sensitive. Sin and sinfulness are not so much the actual doing of things contrary to God's will as the doing of them knowing or thinking them so to be. A man's duty is to obey God, and a virtuous man is a man who has a constant and steady will to obey God. A vicious or sinful man is one who through weakness of will or through deliberate wickedness does that which he knows to be wrong. The form or essence of sin is the wilful disobedience of conscience.

The distinction between formal and material sin is of great importance. A formal sin is any action done which the agent was aware that he ought not to do, or any action omitted which he was aware ought to have been done. It may be, as we have seen, that objectively considered, it was right that the action should have been done or omitted. But nevertheless there is here the form of sin, disobedience of conscience. A material sin is an action which, objectively considered, it is not right to do or to omit but which the agent, through no fault of his own, conscientiously believes he ought to do or omit. In such a case we say of a man that he acted "in all good faith." Thus a formal sin is always blameworthy: it is what we generally mean by sin. A material sin is not blameworthy: it is not an action which can be approved, because it is in fact wrong, yet no stigma attaches to the agent who has only done what he honestly believed right. The employee in the furniture factory who takes the wood in good faith, commits a material sin if the taking of the wood is in fact stealing. If he takes the wood thinking that it is stealing, he commits a formal sin, whether it is in fact stealing or not.

This distinction between formal and material sin, and the attachment of blame only to those actions which are done in violation of conscience, or in obedience to a conscience which is wrong because of the negligence or wilfulness of the agent, is a necessary corollary of the principle that conscience is the guide and norm of moral conduct. Yet it must not be taken to mean that it does not matter much what one does provided that one meant well in doing it. It must always be remembered that actions done in obedience to a conscience which ought to have known better, are formal sins and so blameworthy.

It is certainly true that God judges above all else the motive, and rewards the will which seeks to obey Him. We are told in the Gospel that the publicans and harlots, for whom all sorts of excuses may be made and who, despite their sins—and they are many—may retain a surprising quality of humility and unselfishness, are preferred before the scribes whose exact correctness of behaviour is inspired by pride and hard self-sufficiency. Yet the motive which God thus approves and rewards is the desire to do His will. It is the barest hypocrisy to say that so long as I want and am trying to obey God, it does not matter what I do. The wanting to obey God is a desire to do what in fact God wills, and that desire necessarily includes a desire to find out what that is. Hence it is that Christianity lays the greatest stress on this two-fold duty—always to will to do only what we believe is God's will, and always to search honestly and earnestly to discern what that will is. In other words, there is a duty to obey conscience and a duty to keep conscience informed.

Christian ethics has therefore a double task—to make plain what the will of God is, and to build up a habit of cheerful obedience to that will. There are certain virtues which God wills men to acquire, the possession of which will enable a man to perceive and do that which is pleasing to God. There are certain sins or vicious habits which blunt the perceptiveness of conscience, and destroy the will to obey God. Christian ethics is much concerned with these virtues and vices.

The first virtue is faith, whereby a man believes steadfastly in the love and goodness of God and holds fast by all the articles of the Christian creed. To faith is added hope so that the Christian man trusts in the power of God to give to him and to others the virtues and the happiness which as yet they lack: eagerly he hopes for the fulfilment of God's promises and his heart is set on them. Faith and hope are crowned by love; first, love towards God as the only source of all that is truly and permanently desirable, and secondly, towards man as the child of God and made in His image. These are "the theological virtues"; they have God as their object and they guide and strengthen those who possess them to know and to do the will of God. The four so-called cardinal virtues enable the Christian man so to regulate his conduct in this life that in all things he may give expression to his faith, hope and love for God. He governs himself and behaves towards his fellow-men as one who believes in the righteousness of God, hopes for heaven, and loves God.

The first of the cardinal virtues is justice, which causes him who has it to observe scrupulously all his neighbour's rights and to value them as his own. He loves equity and practises fairness; he hates deceit and fraud. Fortitude enables a man to endure temptation without weakness and to suffer hardship without self-pity. He who has fortitude will not be deflected from the path of duty by any difficulty or danger or evil consequences to himself. Temperance governs and restrains the appetites for pleasure: it confines them within the limits of reasonable enjoyment. The temperate man will not be tempted away from duty by the desires of self-indulgence. And finally prudence, the power of right judgement, enables the Christian man to see clearly where his duty lies; it makes his conscience to be well-informed by careful thought and wisely sought advice and keenly attunes it to catch the word of God in prayer. Thus it forms conscience into a sensitive guide amid the tangled and complex duties of life.

The acquisition of these seven virtues is not a self-centred cultivation of the soul. They are the good life, life according to the will of God. He who consistently seeks to do his duty for God's sake must inevitably acquire them.

The degree to which he possesses them is the measure of his success and faithfulness in performing the religious personal and social duties of his daily life.

The seven root or capital sins are so-called because each of them is the source and parent of a brood of horrid offspring. First among them is pride, the deadly enemy of all true religion. Pride will not admit man's dependence on his Creator; it breeds self-complacency and self-sufficiency. It is the quintessential form of self-centredness. It so wills to excel and to be preferred before all others that it brooks no interference and will submit to none, not even God. Hence it is the cause "of man's first disobedience" and the source of all subsequent sins. For all deliberate sin, which is disobedience to God, springs ultimately from a proud self-centred determination to please one's self. In this sense pride is called the mother of all sins. There are, however, certain sins which are the children of pride in a special sense, since they naturally and inevitably result from pride. They are presumption, false ambition and conceit.

The next root sin is avarice, the excessive and selfish craving for material possessions. St. Paul said that the love of money is the root of all evil and to what sins avarice easily leads we all know well—violence and fraud, fretting anxiety, hardheartedness. The third root sin is lust, more powerful than anything else to corrupt judgement and to sap moral fibre; it renders its victim the prey of vacillating moods, infirm of purpose and inconstant in loyalty. Akin to lust in cause and effect is gluttony, the excessive indulgence in the pleasures of food and drink. This, too, weakens character and darkens judgement. The fifth sin is envy, an offspring of pride, which cannot bear to see another's prosperity, honour or virtue. It issues in all malice and uncharitableness, in gossip and slander. The sixth sin is excessive anger—a fierce, passionate eagerness for revenge, whether there be actual loss of control or whether it take the form of cold-blooded determination. The sins which result from anger of this kind are quarrelsomeness, violence, the nursing of grudges, and all those actions which we associate with the bad-tempered man who is habitually unable to govern his emotions of anger.

The last root sin is that strange and awful thing acedia. Acedia is a sad dejection of spirit, compound of despair and boredom. It finds no good and no pleasure in anything. Its sinfulness lies in its sloth. It makes no effort of the will to rouse itself from the contemplation of its own misery. The modern phrase which best describes it is "browned off." The consequences of it are well-known to those who have to deal with such persons—listlessness, irritability, inconstancy, a general uselessness.

The virtues and the vices of which we have here been speaking are not so much particular actions, good or bad, as habits, temperaments and dispositions. They are the natural or acquired qualities of an agent which make it easy for him to perform good or bad actions. They are, in fact, elements in his character. Christian ethics warns against the seven root sins or vices not only because any single act dictated by them is necessarily sinful, but also because, if a man is not on his guard against them but allows them to become habits, he will find it impossible to obey his conscience, his conscience will itself be warped and his general moral deterioration will proceed with ever increasing pace. Similarly, Christian ethics encourages the practice of the virtues because their possession inevitably strengthens the will to obey conscience, enlightens conscience and makes easy the path towards happy spontaneous goodness.

The detailed treatment of the root sins, their early manifestations, the precautions to be taken against them, and the remedies to be applied, as also the way in which the virtues may be acquired, and how the will may be strengthened and the affections inspired so that we may more easily obey conscience and pass from reluctant obedience out of duty to the spontaneous self-oblation of love ; in a word, how sins are eradicated and the Christian character built up, all this is the subject matter of ascetic theology. In treating of Christian ethics we are more concerned with the informing of conscience. It is our business to consider what is the law of God for man. It will not be possible to consider the whole law, in all its scope and all its detail. We shall only deal with parts of it, laying especial emphasis on one or two subjects of particular significance to this time and place.

CHAPTER III

THE DUTY OF RELIGION

Man's first duty is towards God. Of course, the whole of man's duty is to God. Right conduct is due from man in obedience to God, his creator. We are to love our neighbour, to act rightly, to tell the truth, to live chastely for God's sake, because God commands it. But there are certain duties which are duties towards God in a narrower sense. They are summed up in the commandment "thou shalt love the Lord thy God with all thy heart and with all thy mind and with all thy soul and with all thy strength." They find expression in what are commonly called religious duties.

The command to love God is directed in the first instance not to the emotions but to the will. To love God means to put God first: to prefer His claims before everything else. The man who would rather suffer great financial loss than do something he knows to be wrong, or the man who would rather die than deny God, truly loves God. But the act of will which puts God first includes also an act of will to discipline the emotions and to foster active desire for God. "Set your affections on things above, not on things on the earth." "Where your treasure is, there shall your heart be also." We are to seek and to find in God what is wholly true and noble and desirable.

We are to search for the evidences of God's wisdom and power. We are to reflect upon and be grateful for His providential care and love as well for all mankind as for ourselves in particular. We are to consider the wonder of His self-revelation in Jesus Christ, His will and power to rescue man from sin and error and to lead him to his perfect destiny. We are to recognize both His loving correction of ourselves, and the blessings material and spiritual which He pours upon us. And we are to cherish the "blessed hope of immortality"

THE DUTY OF RELIGION

which we have in Him. In a word we are to worship Him and offer Him the offering of our reason, a "reasonable sacrifice." We are to devote time and attention to a conscious deliberate rational approach to Him, whereby we may enter into a real and living spiritual communion with Him. This is man's first duty as a free rational creature—to turn to God his maker in whose image he is made, in whom he has all his being.

The first religious duty is the practice of private prayer. Private prayer has many purposes; it is expressive of many attitudes of approach to God. In the first place, and chief of all, it is the recognition of man's creaturely nature and of his total dependence upon his Creator. This is what religious people mean when they talk about "surrender." The first thing that a man is doing when he falls on his knees to pray is an admission of his proper place in the scheme of things; an admission, that is, that he is not himself the centre of the universe, but that he owes his very existence, all that he is and all that he has to Another. Thus he is willing and ready to entrust his whole life, his self, to the care and guidance of God who made him. This is surrender, and it is fairly symbolized by the attitude of kneeling to pray.

The surrender which prayer expresses leads naturally to dedication. The man resolves to obey God in all things and to walk in the ways which He sets before him. The status of creature in the nature of things involves the duty of obedience to the will of the Creator. By the very admission, in the act of prayer, that he is a creature a man commits himself to a recognition of his duty of obedience. Every sincere attempt to pray is accompanied by and resolves itself into a humble resolution to lead a good life : that is, to be the kind of creature God made us to be.

Every renewed resolution to obey immediately provokes an awareness of past disobedience. In the act of praying a man submits himself to the judgement of God and is made aware of his inadequacy and weakness; worse, he knows himself convicted of wilful and direct rebellion against God. All genuine prayer is coloured by that emotion and awareness which is fittingly expressed by the cry "Lord have mercy on me, a sinner." The more successful an act of prayer is in concentrating attention upon the presence of God and in detaching the worshipper from the pressing claims upon him of his daily and worldly affairs, the more completely it succeeds in freeing him for a moment from his constant preoccupation with himself, so much the more intensely does it make him aware both of God's perfect holiness and of his own abject unworthiness. He is made to realize not only the utterly indefensible character of his deliberate transgressions, but also his complete inability of himself ever to attain to that inward purity and selfless love which God intends that he shall have.

All Christian worship contains this element of confession. To those who have not experienced prayer, it often appears forced and even hypocritical. It cannot be understood and appreciated apart from its context. And that context is an awareness of the burning purity of God. It is because in prayer man measures himself not against his fellow-men, but against his creator that self-conviction of sin inevitably and instinctively wells up into consciousness and spills over into the cry of "Lord have mercy." Those who do not experience in prayer this sense of guilt have not understood the awful nature of sin ; and that is because they have not opened their minds to the searching demands of God's righteousness which flow from from the inner nature of His Being. "Thou art of purer eyes than to behold iniquity." God is all goodness and in Him is no shadow even of evil. To stand, therefore, in His presence is inevitably to realize with Isaiah that we are "of unclean lips and dwell in the midst of a people of unclean lips." The test of the genuineness of any act of prayer is the awakening of the sense of guilt and of need.

The need is in the first place a need of forgiveness. For an awakening of the sense of guilt leads only to despair if it is not quietened by the assurance of forgiveness. And despair issues either in reckless revolt or in apathy. The first need of which a man becomes conscious when he feels himself guilty is that of forgiveness : the past must somehow be blotted out and the proper relationship between him and God re-established. Side by side with this, however, goes the need for divine aid to maintain this new relationship. Man needs grace to sin no more. He needs the power of God to move his will constantly towards the things that are good and noble and true, to protect him from the enticing lure of all that is bad and base and false. The more he knows of God by prayer, the more he knows his own inability ever to reach that quality of life which he has learnt to love in God, and in consequence the more he relies on the grace of God to make him that which by nature he cannot be.

It is at this point that "petition" enters into prayer. And it naturally forms so large a part of prayer that we are accustomed to think of prayer and petition as synonymous terms. It naturally forms so large a part because, since prayer is a recognition and admission of our dependence on God, it is inevitable that we turn to Him for everything we need and seek His protection from everything we fear. The most important thing which we need is goodness, the thing which we ought most to fear is sin. Consequently it is but natural and right that a man's prayers should constantly be prayers that God will give him this or that virtue, will inspire in him an ever greater desire for this or that kind of nobility, and will strengthen and protect him against this or that temptation. It is the recognition that our very righteousness, such as it is, is wholly given us from God and inspired by Him that inevitably prompts us to pray that He will continue and perfect the good work which He has begun in us. Yet if petitions for grace are properly our first petitions, they are not our only ones. There is nothing wrong in praying for material blessings as well as spiritual. Indeed the very fact of our praying for them is proof and evidence that we confess that they come from God. All good gifts are His. And being wholly dependent on Him it is right that we should ask of Him everything that we need, and everything also that we want : it being always understood that we ask subject to His will. There are many things which we want desperately, believing that they are good and that their possession and enjoyment will enrich our lives. And so we ask God for them.

But if in fact they are not good, or if, though good, we love them too much, then when God denies them we do not rebel. Though we want them, we want still more what He wills for our true good. We ask according to our lights : we accept what He gives.

As we pray for ourselves, so we pray for others. Intercession is a large part of prayer. We would do the best thing possible for our friends, but we know so little even about those we love most that often we do not know what is best for them. In prayer we commit them to God who knows all things, and can do all things. We pray for others as we pray for ourselves : first for their souls' true weal for everything which ennobles and purifies, secondly for their material necessities, and thirdly for their happiness and the satisfaction of their desires. To pray to God for another is to recognize that that other is with us God's creature and the object of His care. Altogether apart from the efficacy of intercessory prayer, from its power, that is, to procure God's blessings for others, prayer hallows and ennobles the friendship and love itself. It is a protection against the selfish element in love, against that which tends towards exploitation, or jealousy or possessiveness. For when we pray for one we love, standing consciously in the presence of God, we are driven to seek and ask for the other's true good. We are forced to think of him for whom we pray as equally with us an immortal soul and the child of God, and the object of God's love. We cannot then consent to use him for our own purposes and our own satisfaction. It is for this reason that marriages seldom break down where husband and wife pray for one another, still less if they pray *with* each other.

It is for this reason also that we are particularly commanded to pray for our enemies. When we take into the presence of God—who is love and who is just, our Father and our Judge—the thought of those whom we hate because of the wrongs they have done us, it is inevitable that the violence of our hatred is quietened. The impulse of vindictiveness and the movement of personal resentment have no place before the eternal God ; they seem too petty. Before Him who died on the cross for sinners they are shamed into silence. Before the common Father of all and the one Judge of all, quarrels between brethren and disputes between fellow-sinners fall away. The mind hears only the divine command, "forgive as you have been forgiven" and the divine prayer "Father forgive them, for they know not what they do."

The last approach to God which prayer expresses is gratitude. It is the necessary consequence of all the rest. God made us, to Him we owe our very self, that we are. His care and wisdom give us all the blessings of this life—beauty of earth and sea and sky, health and sleep, work and play, laughter and love and human friendship, everything indeed for which we cling to life and which makes past memories sweet. And more than all this, far more, are His spiritual gifts; the infinite love and patience with which He forgives our sins and constantly inspires in us new movements and aspirations towards the good; the new life which we have in Christ; the "blessed hope of immortality" proclaimed to us in the death and resurrection of Christ; the fellowship of Christians with Christ and in Christ with one another; all the fruits of the Spirit perceived within ourselves and the only source of our true and lasting happiness; the peace of a good conscience and the quiet of a confident trust in His loving protection; in a word, all the blessings of the Christian religion. The Christian, if he prays at all, cannot be insensible of the debt of gratitude which he owes to God. For the very act of prayer is an acknowledgement of the benefits which he has received, an admission that life, forgiveness and grace are his by God's free gift.

Prayer is due to God—it is a duty implicit in man's creaturehood. Prayer, then, is to be practised for its own sake. It remains a duty, something to be done, however little we feel like it, however great an effort it involves, however meagre its results appear to be. There could be no greater mistake than to suppose that prayer ought always to be spontaneous, the natural outcome of a felt desire, or that it should be valued by the extent to which we are aware that it "does us good." That is like supposing that we need take our hat off to a lady only if we are feeling courteous, or stand for the national anthem only in a mood of patriotic feeling; and that either gesture is only right and valuable because it tends to promote courtesy or patriotism. Whereas taking off one's hat is an act of courtesy, and courtesy is always due from a man to a woman. It is true that the act naturally tends to promote that which it expresses, but even if in particular instances it does not, it still remains a duty. So prayer is due to God and is to be done for its own sake. Nevertheless, as expressive of man's proper attitude to God, it tends to foster and promote that attitude, and its practice is vital to the living of a Christian life and to the building up of a Christian character. It serves our good: yet it is to be done as a duty, for God's sake.

It serves our good, because the true Christian character cannot be built up without it. Christian ethics does not aim at a grudging and laborious obedience to the dictates of conscience. It is not its purpose to lay down a number of rules as God's commandments and require men to conform to them. Its aim goes far beyond this. The pattern of behaviour which it describes, the obedience to conscience which it demands are only steps towards the creation of a character. And that character presupposes and requires a constant dependency upon God. Ethics without prayer tends towards self-sufficiency, complacency and pride. Man is disposed to congratulate himself on his own moral rectitude, and comparing himself with his less conscientious fellows to be content with the standard to which he has attained. He becomes insensible of his faults. Moreover the moral struggle against temptation and towards virtue is a pre-occupation with self. The emphasis and centre of interest is the self. I am ruling, restraining, directing myself. But man's true need is to be released from the self and to be centred on God. To this prayer is the only way. The hall-mark of the Christian character is humility. Humility confesses that all we have and are we owe to God. It confesses how far short we fall of what we might be and by the grace of God we shall be. It relies wholly on that grace. Humility is matched in the Christian character by an earnest longing to imitate Christ.

"Except you become as little children you shall not enter into the Kingdom of God": the humility of child-like dependence is the essential qualification for that love of the things of God which constitutes heaven. The proud and self-sufficient may by great conscientious effort become morally upright. The humble "little ones" of Christ are good almost without knowing it, as relying wholly on Him they press on in His footsteps looking only to Him the beginner and finisher of their faith. Prayer, which sets ever before us the beauty of His example and the holiness of His demands, which continually convicts us of our sins, which daily quickens our spiritual desires and renews our heavenly aspirations is indispensable to the making of a Christian man. Christian ethics is not obedience to an impersonal moral law: it is the giving oneself to a personal God. The work is done by prayer: its fruits are shown in "morality." The whole nature of Christian ethics is totally misconceived when it is represented as a code of conduct. That is "the law" of which St. Paul speaks. It is, rather, a manner of life, an attitude towards God and the self: the attitude that by faith are we "saved" through grace, the attitude, in a word, of prayer.

Hitherto we have spoken of prayer as expressing and fostering the true attitude of total dependence on God. We have had in mind a man's inner prayer-life, the prayers which he utters "in secret" in his closet. But that is not the end of the matter. There is another wide area of prayer—public prayer. The Bible contains the revelation of God's saving activity. A constant characteristic of that activity is that its object is a people, a church. The Old Testament records the creation and the history of a chosen people, the New Testament describes its reconstitution as the Church of Christ. Salvation in the Old Testament is "from the Jews." To them is given the knowledge of the true God and His Law, on them is laid the duty and responsibility of witnessing to Him to the outside world, and by incorporation into them is that outside world to be brought into saving contact with God. The Jews are Israel—the people of God. They worship God as a people, in the mount where He chose to put His

Name, according to a ritual divinely revealed. The New Testament makes plain that the calling and education of the Jews was preparatory to the coming among them of the Son of God who was to be both the glory of His own people Israel and a light to lighten the Gentiles. In and through Him the old distinction of Jews and Gentiles is to disappear, merged into the new all-embracing people of God, the new Israel, the Church.

Membership of the Church is open to all through faith in Christ as the Son of God. To become a member of the Church is to be incorporated into Christ, to be made a living member of His Body. This divinely constituted society, continuous with yet distinct from the chosen people of the Old Testament as the New Covenant supersedes the Old, exists as the Kingdom of God on earth. In it God reigns and dwells. Through it He speaks to the world; it is the organ of His activity, His Body. It is the means by which and the sphere in which He continues the saving work begun at the Incarnation, and makes its fruits perpetually available for each succeeding generation. Further, the Church as the people of God and as the Body of Christ perpetuates the self-offering of Christ in worship and life. The prime task and duty of the Church is to worship God—to offer to God in the name of Christ and with Christ at her head man's due offering of submission, repentance and amendment. This she does in obedience to Christ's command, by offering the perpetual memorial of His Cross and Passion and Resurrection in the Eucharist or Holy Communion. "This do in remembrance of Me."

It follows from all this that the duty of religion includes the duty of being baptised into the Church and thereafter of living as an active member of the Church. God calls us to Himself through Christ, and the Church is the perpetuation of Christ's work on earth. The duties involved in active membership of the Church are these. First and foremost to play one's part in the worship offered by the Church, and particularly at the Eucharist. The Eucharist is a two-way activity. The Church, with Christ at her head, offers to God the memorial of his sacrifice, thus embodying on earth the timeless act of heaven where "He ever liveth to make intercession for us." Thus united with her head in His offering, the life and spirit of Christ flow back into the Church through the sacramental vehicle of the bread and wine. It is the duty of all members of the Church to participate in this common worship, that it may be as complete as possible, and lest the Body grow sickly because its members are not being channels of this spiritual life through sacramental grace. In other words, the duty to be a regular communicant is not so much or not only one to ourselves—a necessity of our own religious life—but one to the whole Church. The same duty obtains, to a lesser extent, to take part in the other public services of the Church. The Church can only perform her prime function of offering worship to God through the worship of her members. It is not that going to Church makes us feel good or edifies us : it is rather that going to Church is a duty we owe to God and to one another. "To forsake the assembling of ourselves together as the manner of some is" argues a certain pride and self-sufficiency together with an indifference that the Church's worship should go on without us and be to that extent imperfect. For in the Body of Christ, no one cell, no one member can take the place or make the offering of another. The Church in heaven is the Communion of Saints—a fellowship—a worshipping community : the Church on earth is of the same nature.

The second duty of churchmanship is the setting of a good example by the cheerful acceptance and willing discharge of the common discipline which the Church imposes on her members. The simple rules of feasts and fasts, the ordering of public worship, the customs of reverence not only have as their object the support of the weaker brethren who are not able to impose a discipline on themselves, they are also a public profession and willing acknowledgement of a common way of life and a common worship. Unmotivated non-conformity with the laws and customs of the religious community to which we belong if it is not mere weakness and self-indulgence, is an offence against charity. It argues a desire for superiority by the parade of a superior knowledge or of a superior discipline ; it suggests a wish to show oneself different from the common herd. Thus it constitutes a denial of the brotherly equality of all members of the Church as children of God. "But if any man seem to be contentious, we have no such custom, neither the churches of God" said St. Paul of those who were unwilling to conform to the custom of women wearing hats in Church. Unnecessary refusal to obey and observe laws and customs is to be contentious and so to sin against unity and love.

Another religious duty is almsgiving. I am not here speaking of almsgiving in general, of that wide general duty of compassion for the weak and of assisting the needy. That duty derives from the second great commandment, to love one's neighbour as one's self, and is laid upon all Christians with particular clarity and emphasis by both the teaching and the example of our Lord. Those who are called by the name of Him who "for us men and for our salvation came down from Heaven" cannot be deaf to His command that "ye love one another as I have loved you. So shall ye be my disciples." I am speaking, here, of a particular kind of almsgiving, namely of acts of charity done indeed to our neighbour—for to whom else can we do them—but done in the name of God and offered to Him. It is, perhaps, artificial thus to distinguish between almsgiving prompted by love of our neighbour, and almsgiving prompted by love of God. For all true Christian love of neighbour is rooted in love of God. We love our neighbour and seek his real good because he is the child of God, and Christian charity differs from ordinary humanitarianism and benevolence because it is directed by an act of will particularly towards the wretched, the outcast, the unrewarding and the unloveable. "If ye love them which love you what reward have ye? Do not even the publicans the same?" The Christian, conscious of the undeserved mercies he has received from God, who "died for us while we were yet sinners," strives to imitate God especially in this, by helping the helpless, giving without thought of reward and loving where there is little to love. The distinction between the two kinds of almsgiving is certainly not one to be pressed, and it may be that all true Christian almsgiving is a specifically religious act.

Nevertheless it remains true that there are some kinds of almsgiving which are more easily recognized as directly religious and of which God rather than man appears to be more immediately the object. They may be summed up in the phrase "Church work." There are, for example, many charitable organizations which are created and maintained by religious communities in the name of God. To contribute to such organizations is to give to God. Or again, through the missionary societies the Church carries out her duty to preach the gospel throughout the world. To give to the missionary societies is to give to God that His name may be hallowed, His Kingdom come. To support schools where a religious education is provided is likewise to give to God. To maintain the work of the Church in any form and in any place, as, for example, to contribute to the maintenance of the clergy, or to help build, endow or equip a place of worship is to give to God to promote His glory.

What distinguishes this kind of almsgiving from almsgiving in general is its motive. This is a desire to give something directly to God for His glory and His work. It is an expression of our knowledge that all we have is from God and that of His own we give Him. This found its simplest and most direct expression in the old system of tithes: to-day the widespread popularity of the harvest festival witnesses to the same profound instinct and desire. It is directly religious since it springs from an acknowledgement of our creaturely dependence on God, and is a gesture and symbol of our self-dedication to God. The gift represents the giver: it is like a sacrifice. It is given not so much because we love our neighbour and it will benefit him, as because we love God, and in giving symbolise that we give ourselves.

The Christian tradition has always recognized three preeminent religious duties—prayer, almsgiving and fasting. This third duty is not perhaps much thought of nowadays. From the time of the Reformation it has been a constant object of attack and even ridicule. Special times of fasting and legally obligatory forms of self-denial have been described as the essence of formalism, and as the supreme exaltation of works over grace. They have been dismissed as a parody of the true religious life and as a ridiculous pre-occupation with trivialities. It is true that the more serious objectors to the Church's rules of fasting have never underrated the value of fasting in itself, and have themselves lived lives of disciplined self-denial and even austerity. Yet the cumulative effect of their objections has been that a general ignoring of the Church's prescribed times and rules has led to a general neglect of the duty to fast itself.

The practice of fasting is a common-place of the Bible. Our Lord fasted Himself and assumed that His followers would fast. "When the bridegroom is taken away from them, then shall they fast in those days" (Mark ii, 20), and "Moreover, when ye fast, be not as the hypocrites of a sad countenance" (Matthew vi, 16). Fasting is not the same as self-denial and self-discipline. It differs both in content and motive. In content it is a particular kind of self-denial and discipline; for it consists in a regulated use of food, and is not concerned with anything else. The details of the regulated use, the extent and the seasons of fasting which from time to time have been or are now imposed by religious authorities is not a proper subject for discussion here. We are more concerned with the general duty and its motive.

This motive is not simply the acquisition and practice of self-control. Fasting, as a religious duty is something done directly for God's sake. It is a religious activity in three senses. First, to deny one's self food is to discipline the body and bring it under subjection that it may be a docile instrument in God's service. Second, the practice of fasting is an open recognition that bodily and so all earthly pleasures and even necessities are secondary. The things of God are of the first importance. The practice of fasting impresses on men that there is nothing which may not have to be sacrificed in the service of God, and is itself a token of surrender; a token of the readiness of the will to forsake all and follow Him. That is to say, the practice of fasting expresses and inculcates that detachment which is characteristic of the properly Christian use of earthly pleasures and possessions. Thirdly, and perhaps most important, fasting like almsgiving is a form of direct giving to God. It can be an expression, sometimes the only possible expression, of our desire to make amends for past sin. It can be an evidence of our willingness to have a share in His sacrifice, a token of our readiness to give ourselves to Him, to give all that we have and are. Because fasting is in one or all of these ways an act directed towards God, a giving of the body to God, it develops humility: for it expresses our creatureliness, that we owe life itself to God. Its religious value is attested by countless generations. There is great need in our day for the Church to teach this duty more emphatically, to explain its nature, and, for the benefit of the weaker brethren, to impose by rule a minimum of obligation. When all Christians fast, and fast together, they confess dramatically their common belief in God as their Creator and their common recognition that they do but exist to do Him service.

Religion, which finds expression in these various ways, is the first duty of man. "Thou shalt love the Lord thy God. . ." This love is shown by giving to God of our substance, by loyal obedience to the good laws and reasonable customs of the religious community to which we belong, and above all by worship, both at home and in Church. The first and fundamental demand of God is that we worship Him. We are to seek and to find in Him what is wholly true and noble and desirable. We are to let ourselves rest content with nothing less. Measuring ourselves by the standard of His known demands, we are to confess our own selfish wickedness and our utter inability, of ourselves, to attain that inward purity and love which he intends that we shall have. Thus, knowing our own sinful state, we are to rely wholly upon His saving mercy, constantly to implore His healing grace and thankfully receive it as He pours it out in response to our prayer and worship. Thus to seek and to acknowledge God in private and public worship, and to receive the sacraments of His grace is man's first duty. Careful attention to this will produce in a man a sharp awareness of his other duties and a readier will to perform them.

These other duties are summed up in the sentence "Thou shalt love thy neighbour as thyself." No man is born to himself alone. It is man's nature and God's will that he should live in society. Only so can he reach his own perfection. By promoting the welfare, by maintaining the peace, harmony and order of society he serves both his neighbour and himself. The first, then, of the Christian man's duties, after religion, which we shall consider is the duty to obey the law.

CHAPTER IV

THE DUTY OF OBEDIENCE

It may, perhaps, seem strange to say that the first of our duties towards our neighbour is to obey the law. Yet it is not without significance that in the Ten Commandments the first four deal with our duty to God and the last six with our duty to our neighbour, and that of these last six, the first commands respect to parents. That is to say, the first of the neighbour-commandments is concerned with the natural authority of parents within the family. The family is the basic unit of human society. The principle of authority and the consequent duty of obedience, inherent in the structure of the family, holds good in all the societies in which men are grouped. It has been a constant element in Christian ethics, from the time of the Roman emperors until to-day, that by the will of God men owe obedience to lawful authority "for conscience sake." Nowhere, perhaps, has this been more constantly taught than in England. And at no time in English history, perhaps, has it been more strikingly illustrated than in the writings of Christian divines in the troubled times of the Civil War, in the days of Charles I. In order, therefore, to get a clear and vivid picture of this supremely important part of Christian teaching on the duty of the citizen to the State and on the virtue of obedience, it will be well worth while to listen to these ancestors of ours, who lived in times not altogether unlike our own and who experienced dangers and disasters similar to those which threaten us.

It was in 1647 that Robert Sanderson, then Regius Professor of Divinity, delivered a course of lectures at Oxford on "The Obligation of Conscience." Much of these lectures was devoted to this subject. The Professor, soon to be deprived for a while of his stall and his chair, discoursed on the divine authority of kings, on the duty of subjects to obey, or if not to obey then to suffer, on the final iniquity and blind destructive folly of rebellion. In the troubled times in which he lived it seemed to him self-evident that, saving the overriding rights of conscience, the first duty of the citizen is obedience. Only by insistence on this duty could the door be firmly shut against faction, selfish ambition and restless discontent. Once undermine this virtue of obedience and it is all up with the peace and order of society, the bloodshed and rapine of civil wars become inevitable.

Nor was his voice alone in that disturbed generation. There was then a little school of English moral theologians. They are all at one in this insistence on the prime importance of the virtue of obedience. Robert Sanderson was a Canon of Christ Church and later Bishop of Lincoln. His contemporary Richard Baxter was a curate at Kidderminster under the Establishment, but a man of independent views and indeed, in all but name, an Independent. His "Directions for subjects concerning their duty to their rulers" contains these words: "Begin with an absolute universal obedience to God, your Creator and Redeemer. . . . Having begun with God, obey your governors as the officers of God, with an obedience ultimately divine." (*Christian Directory*, Book IV, Cap. 3.) William Ames was a Calvinist and professed Nonconformist. He too teaches that the power of the magistrate is supreme, that it is instituted by God, that all subjects should pray for their governors, honour and reverence them, and owe to them subjection and obedience (*De Conscientia* v, 25). The common foundation of this common teaching is that "the powers that be are ordained of God," whence it follows that obedience to them is a moral duty and that human laws bind the conscience.

The influence of this teaching on English life has been immense. Continuously sustained through many generations, enshrined in the Church Catechism, preached from the pulpit, taught in the homes of the people, it has contributed very greatly to the reputation which the English enjoy of being a law-abiding, law-respecting nation. It is a very disturbing aspect of our contemporary religious life that this teaching seems now to be out of fashion and to be obsolescent. The modern fever for equality, independence and liberty makes

THE DUTY OF OBEDIENCE

this teaching very unpalatable, no doubt; yet it is almost as badly needed now as in the seventeenth century, when there was also a fever for liberty and independence and equality.

In every branch of life there is a prevailing temper of disobedience. The true nature of obedience and submission is scarcely known. Men are prepared to obey only where they understand, approve and like. To obey for the sake of obedience, to obey when we see no need, or when it is inconvenient and unpleasant, or, still more, when it is unfair is thought to be servile, an offence against human dignity, a denial of manly independence. This temper starts in the home, where the disobedience of children to their parents nowadays is notorious. The juvenile courts are crowded with delinquents whose parents confess that they cannot control them. These children are not taught obedience as a duty, nor does a sentimental age allow their schoolmasters the use of the rod to teach them manners. They are from the first deprived of instruction in what is the fundamental prerequisite for life in an ordered society, namely to do one's duty in one's own sphere and place, and not to meddle in other men's duties and play their part instead of one's own.

The same temper of disobedience is to be found in the factories. It appears that no direction can be enforced unless it is accompanied by interminable explanations and exhortations, by conferences at floor-level and every other level. And even then it seems that any orator can easily convince any audience that a particular order is unjust or unnecessary and therefore ought to be disobeyed. One might think that no one had ever heard of the general duty in all walks of life to obey those that are set in authority. And it is probably true that the majority has never heard. It is not that there is anything wrong in explaining the justice or necessity of particular orders, or anything wrong in the demand for such explanation. The error lies in the unquestioned assumption that orders carry with them no obligation to obey unless and until they be approved by those who are to obey them. And even that is not all. The temper of disobedience has spread so far that even when approval has been sought and obtained in the only possible way, through representatives, those representatives are themselves disobeyed. There is no understanding of the fact that in every society of men, once its officers are appointed or elected, authority over the members of that society in all things which affect that society passes to them, and obedience becomes due. If it is not so, if the members do not recognize the authority of their own officers, but try to keep the authority in their own hands, then the society has no head, is incapable of directing its affairs, and collapses into a mere aggregate of individuals. If men are to live in societies, they must yield obedience to the heads of those societies. It is written in nature. A society is, by definition, an association of men in a common purpose or a common life under a common head or direction.

It is not surprising that there are now signs that this prevailing temper of disobedience is spreading into the sphere of the State. Heavy taxation and the multiplicity of laws and orders regulating the market and industry have caused the law to press hardly on individuals who before were scarcely aware of its existence. There are ominous signs of a widespread tendency to question the justice or necessity of these laws, and to deny their obligation when they are found to be inconvenient. It is becoming a common opinion that there is no moral duty to obey these laws, and that all are entitled to evade them if they can. Laws which enforce on the citizen an unwelcome austerity are bound in the nature of things to constitute a severe strain on loyal obedience. It becomes more than ever necessary to sound a recall to the duty of obedience, and to re-teach the old lesson that the welfare of the community presupposes and rests upon respect for authority : because in the nature of things and by the command of God, man is a "political animal" and owes obedience to his governors.

Unfortunately the Church of England, whence this re-call should sound, is in no position to utter it. She is herself infected with this malaise of disobedience. It is not improbable that it is for this reason that she has allowed the virtue of obedience to be so little taught lately, and that again, for this reason, her hold on the people has lessened and the people have thus lapsed into disobedience. For the Church is in a condition of lawlessness. Her clergy do not obey the laws by which she is administered. There are reasons for this. As far back as 1906 a Royal Commission declared that the ecclesiastical law was too narrow and rigid for the contemporary needs of the Church. Only a handful of the clergy are malignantly disloyal or in wilful perversity contemptuous of the law. As a whole, the clergy are disobedient either because the law is impossible of fulfilment, or in obedience to the scriptural warrant to obey God rather than man, that is, for conscience sake. But the effect of this example has been disastrous. If only for the sake of its own self-preservation, the State should see to it at once that the Church has freedom to reform herself so as to produce a body of law which can be and would be obeyed. The task of reforming the canon law which is now before the Convocations is of national importance, because on its success depends the beginning of a recovery of order and obedience within the Church. And that recovery would mean much for the renewal of the spirit of obedience throughout the nation. For as the clergy hear again the call to submission and find themselves once again under a law to which they can and should give conscientious obedience, so they will again begin to teach their people the duty of obedience as it has always been taught by the Christian religion.

Christian ethics has consistently held that this duty rests upon divine commandment: and that in two senses. It is both written in Scripture and taught by nature; it is at once revealed divine law and natural law. That the duty of obedience which children owe to parents is part of the natural law is clear enough. Baxter provides us with a good example of this side of Christian teaching in Book II, Cap. xi, Section 3 of his *Christian Directory*. Addressing the children, he says: "Remember, that as nature hath made you unfit to govern yourselves, so God in nature hath mercifully provided governors for you. . . . Consider also that your parents' government is necessary to your own good. . . . As your bodies would have perished if your parents or some others had not taken care of you when you could not help yourselves, so your minds would be untaught and ignorant, even like brutes, if you had not others to teach and govern you. Nature teacheth the chickens to follow the hen, and all things when they are young to be led and guided by their dams, or else what would become of them?"

But just as parents and parental authority are essential to the well-being and education of the young, so the state and civil authority are essential to the well-being and development of the grown man. Civil authority is necessary for the stability and harmony of society; a stable and harmonious society provides the best environment for the living of a true and full human life. Civil authority, therefore, is natural, that is, required by the nature of man for its proper development. Thus we find that Sanderson, when discussing the duty of a citizen towards a usurper, argues that although the laws of a usurper have no moral force in themselves, because the usurper has no just authority to make laws, nevertheless, within certain limits, the citizen has a moral duty to obey them. And he gives as one of his reasons, this: "No man is born for himself alone, but for the human race and the public good: hence arises the third necessity for obeying the powers that be, no matter by what means they attained to power. And hence we may infer the limit of that obedience which is due in conscience. Whatever is done for the sake of something else, must be done so far as it still seems necessary and useful for the attainment of that end. The end of government and of the obedience due to it is the peace and safety of human society. . . . For this three things are above all necessary: first defence against external enemies, secondly the administration of law whereby the good are rewarded and the wicked punished, and thirdly the management of trade and business. With these three things the safety of the human race is so bound up that in their absence everything inevitably goes to rack and ruin. . . . There is only one remedy, for good citizens to remember that it is their duty to obey those who in fact wield authority in everything which makes for the public safety." (*De Consc.* v, 19.) In other words, society, and in society authority is necessary, in the nature of things, for human well-being.

This teaching of nature is amply reinforced by scripture. "Honour thy father and thy mother." "By Me kings reign and princes decree justice." "There is no power but of God; the powers that be are ordained of God. Whosoever therefore resisteth the power, resisteth the ordinance of God." "Submit yourselves to every ordinance of man for the Lord's sake." "Servants be subject to your masters with all fear: not only to the good and gentle, but also to the froward." "But the thing," says Jeremy Taylor, the Restoration Bishop, "is expressly affirmed by the Scripture: for having dogmatically and fully signified that all human just power is of God . . . it is not content to leave us to find out the consequence, but literally affirms the main articles. So St. Peter 'Be ye subject to every ordinance of man for the Lord's sake' which St. Paul speaks yet more explicitly 'Wherefore it is necessary that ye be subject not only for wrath but also for conscience sake.' Nothing can add light to these so clear words, they are bright as the sun, certain as an article of faith, clear, easy and intelligible, according to the nature of universal Divine commandments. St. Chrysostom and Theodoret urging these precepts, say that we are not to obey out of courtesy but of duty, not out of liberality but necessity; that is, according to St. Ambrose and St. Austin, the fearful pains of hell and eternal damnation attend them that disobey." (*Duct. Dub.*, III, Cap. i, No. 12.)

This teaching is the authoritative voice of Christendom. It means that lawful human authority and power is part of the divine intention. Side by side with the truths that all men are equal in their common humanity and that every individual is of infinite worth in himself, stands this other truth that as members of societies men are not equal; it is the part of some to govern and command, of others to be governed and to obey. This is true not only of the citizen and the state; it holds also of smaller and private relationships. "By human laws," says Sanderson, "are to be understood not only the public laws of communities . . . but also the particular commands of parents, masters and all other superiors to their children, servants and subordinates. . . . So far as its obligatory force and effect is concerned every kind of legislative power, both public and private is ordered of God." (*De Consc.* v, 4.)

The effect of this is that human law binds the conscience. In consequence to do what law forbids or omit what law commands is not merely a crime but a sin. Where positive human law prescribes or particularizes the moral law, this presents no difficulty. There is an obvious moral obligation not to commit murder or theft. Difficulty arises over those human laws—and they are the majority—which concern actions in themselves and apart from these laws morally indifferent. How can it be true that to park my car in Oxford Street or sell my potatoes for more than the legal maximum price is sinful?

The older casuists were not unaware of this problem. It was frequently objected to them that this doctrine of obedience confers upon men that power of binding conscience which properly belongs to God alone. It is not for men, but only for God to make and declare actions to be sinful. The consistent reply to this objection was that human law binds the conscience not directly but indirectly. That is to say, an action otherwise indifferent or even good which the law forbids, does not become intrinsically evil because of the law; it is evil indirectly, because to do it is an act of disobedience when God has commanded obedience. It is not the action in itself, but the disobedience which is sinful. For example, the present controls and restrictions which govern the world of commerce are just laws in so far as they are, as a whole and in general, necessary to the good of society. Yet it cannot be said of many of the particular transactions which they forbid that they are, singly and individually, so necessary: that is, it cannot be said of each and every such transaction that it is, and of its very nature must be, an offence against society. The sinfulness of the black market—or at least of the grey market—lies precisely and solely in its illegality, in its being disobedient to lawful authority.

The point is made clear in Jeremy Taylor when he discusses the conditions which excuse a citizen from obedience, and gives this illustration. "As if a law be made that corn shall not be transported, because of an imminent famine . . .

if any man to save his life shall . . . carry some abroad, his necessity is a just excuse . . . though every single man must not pretend that his single proportion will be no great matter (because that is not sufficient unless there be a great necessity to do it). . . . Other men cannot say, why may not I as well as he? Unless the necessity be as exemplary as the action . . . they cannot pretend to the like impunity." (*Duct. Dub.*, III, i, Rule II, 17.) That is to say the breach of a law of this kind may be no great matter in itself, it may harm nobody, or harm them very little. Nevertheless, there is a moral obligation to obey.

This obligation of human law upon conscience is essential to good government and stable society. No government can be so omniscient and so vigilant that it can everywhere always enforce obedience to its laws by the fear of punishment alone. The efficiency of laws depends chiefly and ultimately upon the citizens' recognition that they are bound in conscience to obey them. Once this is gone, once public opinion tolerates or approves widespread evasion and disobedience, the fabric of society is loosened. It is above all things essential to impress firmly upon all classes of society the over-riding general duty of obedience to lawful authority as a matter of common morality.

All the same, it is not possible to maintain that every breach of every human law is sinful. In the first place it is universally admitted that no one is bound to obey a law when obedience will bring about his ruin. Laws are meant to benefit and protect the subject, not to destroy him. And although in some cases it may be necessary to obey even at the risk of death—as the soldier may not desert his post in time of danger—yet in general it is conceded that human laws do not oblige the conscience "where there is an imminent danger of death, or an intolerable or very grievous evil in the obedience." (Taylor, ibid. III, i, Rule II.)

But such cases are naturally rare. A far greater problem is raised by the fact that there are many laws of which common sense and public opinion will never admit that they carry with them any moral obligation. The clearest examples of such laws are provided by police regulations and municipal bye-laws, such as the prohibition to park a car in a certain thoroughfare, to ride a bicycle without a rear light, or to walk on the grass. Such regulations concern actions which are highly inconvenient when performed by great numbers of people, but of no consequence if they are done occasionally and by few. The ordinary man feels no sense of guilt when he breaks any of them. The reason for this is that he does not believe that those who make these regulations have any intention of imposing a moral obligation to obey them. And the obligation of a law does not extend beyond the intention of the law-giver to oblige. If, therefore, the law-giver does not intend to bind the conscience, then the conscience is not bound. It is the general view that in the laws of the police-regulation type there is a tacit understanding that what those who make them intend is that people shall either obey them or pay a penalty for disobeying them. And they make the penalty severe enough to ensure that few people will think it worth while to run the risk of incurring it. They rely, that is, on the deterrent force of the penalty without imposing any moral obligation. Laws of this kind are known as "purely penal" laws: there is no sin in disobeying them, the only duty involved is that of submitting to the penalty if it is imposed.

There is no doubt that laws of this kind exist. And they form an exception to the general rule that obedience to law is a moral obligation. Yet it is very difficult to be certain which they are. It is held by some people that because modern legislation rarely, if ever, explicitly states that the law is to be obeyed as a matter of duty, but is content to set out the penalties which will be incurred by disobedience, therefore most modern laws are purely penal. There is no evidence, they say, that the legislators take the slightest interest in the consciences of their subjects or have any intention of imposing any moral obligations. This is an exaggerated and untenable position. If it were true it would mean that everybody was free to disobey almost any law if he liked, and an impossible strain would be imposed on the police force to detect and punish offenders. Whilst it may be probable that in some few and relatively unimportant matters authority is indifferent whether people obey or not, and is content to rely on the penalty to bring about general obedience, it is incredible that they should intend this in general and about most matters. The presumption lies the other way, and no law may properly be regarded as purely penal unless there is overwhelming evidence that it is so. The general assumption must be that authority intends the law to be conscientiously obeyed and to that end imposes on everyone a moral obligation to obey it.

The customs laws furnish an interesting example of this kind of problem. There are many people who see no harm in evading customs if they can, and regard the whole business as a battle of wits between themselves and the customs officers. This is because they hold that the authorities do not forbid the importing of certain articles, but impose a charge on those who import them. The only moral obligation, therefore, which arises is that of paying the dues if and when they are demanded. If they are not demanded, there is no obligation to pay them. It may well be that this is the correct view, and that the authorities are, in fact, perfectly indifferent whether people import nothing or whether they import and pay. In that case there is nothing wrong in smuggling things through the customs if one can. That is to say, it would be legitimate to conceal things, or to slip across the frontier in such a way as to avoid the customs officers. It would not, of course, be legitimate to do anything in itself wrong in the interests of evasion; for example, it would not be legitimate to tell a direct lie in answer to a direct question. But perhaps we have taken this piece of casuistry far enough.

Only it ought to be added that there is one further consideration which would make the customs laws different from other penal laws—if they are penal laws. Customs are lawful taxes, and most people hold that there is a moral obligation to pay lawfully imposed taxes whether they are demanded or not. This is the explanation of those occasional acknowledgements of "conscience money" by the Chancellor of the Exchequer. Some people, when they find that they have been asked for and paid less tax than they are legally liable to pay, feel themselves under an obligation to pay the additional difference. If this view is correct, there is a duty to make a full voluntary declaration and to offer to pay the customs even when they are not demanded. In this the customs laws, if they are penal, would differ from other penal laws. In the case of other penal laws it is agreed that there is no obligation to pay the fine or penalty unless and until it is demanded.

Penal laws, then, constitute an exception to the general rule. The general rule is that to be law-abiding—to obey the law because it is the law—is a Christian duty, since "the powers that be are ordained of God" and the laws which they make, they make and impose with the authority of God. It is as the ministers of God that obedience is due to them. This introduces an important qualification in the duty to obey the law, for it pre-supposes that the authorities, being the ministers of God, act justly. In so far as they act unjustly they are not His ministers. Unjust laws, therefore, impose no sort of obligation on the conscience to obey them.

This corollary preserves the Christian doctrine of obedience from the charge that it fosters servility and betrays the inviolable rights of conscience. The subject owes obedience to the commands of his superior only in so far as those commands are just. It might seem that the proviso takes away everything that the doctrine of obedience had given; for it makes the subject sit in judgement on the superior, and requires him to obey only if he thinks his superior is acting justly. It requires therefore very careful handling, and all moral theologians devote considerable space to a consideration of what makes a law unjust.

It is clear, in the first place, that if the law-giver has no lawful authority, or exceeds his authority, his commands cannot carry with them any moral obligation. Actions which are ultra vires have no power over conscience. Nevertheless, as we have seen, in Sanderson's judgement—though not all would agree with him—the citizen ought to obey the laws of an usurped authority within certain limits. Laws which are essential to the peace and integrity of society should be obeyed for the sake of society. This is a problem which was raised in an acute form during the war for some countries by the fact of enemy occupation. The problem is, of course, how far, if at all, is it my duty to obey the orders of the occupying power? The underground movements, in so far as they acted on the principle that it was legitimate to disobey any and every law made by the illegal occupying authority would not have met with Sanderson's approval. He would have urged the duty of obedience not only to the moral law but also to such other laws as were essential to the peaceful ordering of society.

It is also clear in the second place, that a law may be unjust because it does not serve the public good. To promote the public good is the proper purpose and justification of all law. It is also clear in the third place, that a law may be unjust because it is unfair in the duties it demands from particular individuals or in the burden which it imposes on them. The casuists are not agreed about the moral obligation of such laws. Sanderson, for example, maintains that though such laws are unjust and involve those who make them in sin, nevertheless subjects are still bound to obey them; for it is not the business of subjects to determine what does or does not serve the public good or what is or is not an equal distribution of burdens. (*De Consc.* vi, 14.) Others maintain, however, that although the subject may, if he likes, obey such laws, he is under no obligation to do so. He does not sin, if he disobeys. But to this rule they also add an important qualification. He must be morally certain that the law is unjust, and must not, by his disobedience, set an example of lawlessness, bring authority into public contempt, or incite others to disobey. In the words of Jeremy Taylor (*Duct. Dub.*, III, Cap. i, Rule 3) the law is not to be disobeyed "with the scandal and offence of others, it must be so done that none be taught to rebel or evacuate the law upon pretences and little regards, nor that our duty and religion be evil spoken of, nor that the superior be made jealous and suspicious."

Finally, and most important of all, a law may be unjust because it commands something which is positively immoral. Here the subject's duty is clear. He must obey God rather than man. Not only is he under no obligation to obey, he has an absolute duty to disobey. All the moral theologians are perfectly clear about this. They are at one in denouncing any doctrine of blind obedience. They insist that it is every man's duty to scrutinise the laws before he obeys them, in case they should command something evil. And they imperatively demand that if the law is evil it must be disobeyed.

Yet they were keenly alive to the danger to peace and order which the recognition of the essential liberty of conscience involves. They met this danger by insisting on the one hand that though the subject must disobey, yet he must not resist, and on the other hand by requiring a certainty that the law is unjust before admitting the morality of disobedience. The laws are not to be disobeyed "upon pretence and little regards." There must be more than a mere scruple or a hair-splitting objection.

The law must be manifestly and notoriously unjust, or at the least, after careful enquiry and thought, the subject must be morally certain that the law is unjust before he can safely disobey it. "For it is no warranty to disobey," says Taylor (ibid. No. 12) "that I fancy the law to be unjust: and therefore in this case the best security we can have is, that either it be so declared by the voice of all men or the more sober accents of the wise men, or be evident in itself according to the strictest measures." And further, so long as the subject only doubts that the law is just, and is not sure of its injustice, the moral obligation to obey remains. For the presumption is in favour of the Government. It is to be assumed, until in any case it is found otherwise, that the Government does its duty and only orders what is right or in the public interest. Proper respect for authority demands this. To hold otherwise, to assume upon every serious doubt, that the law is more probably unjust than just, is to hold the government in contempt. As this is in general contrary to order and so to the common good, so also it is expressly forbidden in Scripture—we are not to speak evil of dignities.

Though the theologians admit the duty of reproving authority for its injustices and of criticizing its unjust laws, they are not always clear as to whose duty it is. On the whole they prefer to lay greater emphasis on the general duty of most people in most circumstances to refrain from open criticism. They were writing for the English, and there was little need to encourage the English to rebuke authority for wrong-doing. There was more need to teach the duty of respect. "Meddle not uncalled with the matters of superiors, and take not upon you to censure their actions, whom you have neither ability, fitness or authority to censure. How commonly will every tradesman and labourer at his work be censuring the councils and government of the King and speaking of things which they never had means sufficiently to understand?" (*Christian Directory*, IV, iii, No. 38.) The words of the independent Baxter fall somewhat strangely on our modern ears. Yet however appropriate free and vigorous criticism may be to a politically mature community, it all too easily degenerates into cheap and facile disparagement. No society is likely to remain for long law-abiding once it has lost its respect for authority. Hostile criticism of those who hold authority passes by easy stages into hostile rejection of the authority which they hold. And that authority is of God. For "By Me kings reign and princes decree justice."

CHAPTER V

SOCIAL DUTIES

Our first duty towards our neighbour is then a duty of obedience to authority in the interests of stable human society. It is a duty to society. All the remaining duties may be summed up as different aspects of the duty to respect our neighbour's rights. And this itself is derived from the duty to promote and maintain peaceful social intercourse among men within a society. And this duty is laid upon us by God who has ordained and so created us that we grow to our full maturity not as isolated individuals but as members of a community. It may seem strange to sum up a man's duty to his neighbour as a duty to respect his rights when the Bible says that love is the fulfilment of the law and that the summary of the law is that "thou shalt love the Lord thy God . . . and they neighbour as thyself." Rights and love seem far apart. But it is not so.

Every man, by nature, wants the best for himself. He wants his own perfect and eternal happiness. We are to want each other's perfect happiness just as much. As God desires the perfection of every human being that He has created, so we are to desire the self-same thing. All our duties to ourselves and to our fellow-men derive from this. We know that every human being is created by God for an eternal destiny, to become a fully-developed person. Every human being has, therefore, a right to those things which are the necessary condition for his attaining that eternal destiny. Our duty to love our neighbour can thus properly be defined as a duty to respect his rights. These necessary conditions are manifold and various and to each of them every man has a right. For example, he has a right to worship God freely ; he has a right to choose his own wife and to beget children from her, that in the close intimacy of the family he may develop his natural instincts of love and service ; he has a right to form friendships and to join societies that he may similarly develop his natural desire for social intercourse and mutual sympathy and understanding; he has a right, short of the invasion of the equal rights of others, to the free and unmolested use and enjoyment of his physical and mental powers; he has a similar right to the use and enjoyment of his possessions. Our duty to our neighbour is to respect these rights; to do what is in our power to preserve and to promote the conditions which make for his true happiness and never wilfully to hinder them. This is the basis which underlies the virtues of justice and of charity to men. Our duty to our neighbour is compact of justice and love, in imitation of God. Of justice, in that we carefully respect his rights to the things necessary to the attainment of true happiness. Of love, in that we actively promote these rights by an especial care for the weak, the handicapped, the needy and the defenceless.

The underlying and fundamental human rights are protected by the prohibitions of the Ten Commandments. Every man has a right to life and therefore to the free use and disposition of his body in which that life is contained and expressed. The sixth commandment, "Thou shalt not kill," extends beyond murder to forbid all physical assault and violence and all forcible restraint of bodily liberty. To attack another man, to maim him, or to shut him up, are violations of the right to possess one's body. If we are not in full possession of our bodies, able to go where we like and do what we like, if we have not power to use all its limbs and faculties, then we are to that extent hindered and cramped in living a full life and arriving at the goal of a mature developed personality.

It is, of course, true that no man has absolute freedom to go where he likes and to do what he likes. He is conditioned and limited by time and space, and by the pressure and conflict of other duties—for example, to earn his living; the important thing is that within the area allowed by circumstance every man should have the free disposition of his body. To be attacked, restrained, injured or maimed is to be robbed of the right to live our life in our own way, and to the best of our power, just as to be murdered is to be robbed of the right to life itself. It is also true that the right to life and the right to the free disposition of our bodies may be forfeited by crime. That is, an unjust violation of the rights of others may involve us in a just deprivation of our own rights. This is true of all rights. They exist, and are to be respected, but always with due regard to the rights of others.

The seventh commandment, "Thou shalt not commit adultery," protects the rights of the family. Every man and woman has the right, if they choose to exercise it, of marrying and of finding in the union of two lives their mutual development and enrichment. Having chosen to marry, on the one hand no one has the right to come between them or separate them, on the other hand, each has the right to demand and expect of the other complete loyalty and fidelity. "Thou shalt not commit adultery" goes beyond the prohibition of ordinary marital infidelity, and demands of both partners in marriage complete loyalty in thought and word and deed. It also forbids to all others every attempt to disrupt and break up the marriage. In particular it enjoins that chastity and purity which will not allow another person to be used merely as a means of gratifying our own physical desires, as a vessel for our lust. To use others so is to degrade them from the status of persons to that of instruments or things. The prohibition of adultery is a command to purity, to a respect for the bodies and persons of others as existing in their own right and for their own end and not created for our pleasure and enjoyment. It is a command to purity not only in act but also in thought. "But I say unto you that whosoever looketh on a woman to lust after her hath committed adultery with her already in his heart." It is a command to respect the rights of all other persons to be treated as persons and not as things, even in thought, as well as deed. It is a command also to respect the rights which husband and wife have in each other ; a command addressed both to husband and wife themselves and to all others. It proclaims the inviolability of the family from without, and forbids its betrayal from within.

The ninth commandment, "Thou shalt not bear false witness," protects the right to reputation, respect and honour.

Every man is entitled to enjoy a good reputation if he deserves it, and to live in peace among his neighbours, free from hostility and suspicion. Libel, slander and malicious gossip, being destructive of a man's fame and reputation, are an unjust deprivation of his rights. To tell lies about others, so that they become unpopular or so mistrusted that people will not trade with them or employ them, or so that they are unjustly punished for crimes which they have not committed is not only uncharitable but unjust. It robs of a right; the right to a good name. Since man naturally develops as a member of a society, the good esteem of that society, the friendliness of his neighbours, the respect they pay him and the liking they have for him contribute greatly to his development. And he has a right to them. It is a common experience to observe the quick expansion of qualities and powers in a man who finds himself among friends in a congenial environment, compared with the slow, painful, tortuous growth of one who is out of tune with his surroundings and in hostile company. The right, therefore, to enjoy a good reputation which this commandment protects is a very important one.

The eighth and tenth commandments, "Thou shalt not steal" and "Thou shalt not covet," safeguard the rights of property. They proclaim the right of every man to the free use and enjoyment of the things which he possesses. The Christian tradition maintains that among the rights of men is the right to the private ownership of material things. It holds that this is just and consonant with the order of nature. It is worth while to state at some length the Christian justification of the right to property.

It may at first seem surprising to say that the ownership of private property is consonant with the order of nature. Because nature does not divide her gifts between private persons; they are bestowed upon man and only appropriated by individuals. This suggests that the natural order is one in which everything is "wild," belonging to nobody; as the blackberries and primroses in an English roadside hedge are wild, waiting to be picked by anyone who needs or desires them. And it is probable that in the first days of the human race it was like this, and man got his food, as the animals do, where he could find it, living, as we say, from hand to mouth. But human development quickly brought with it private property: indeed, the institution of private property, which enabled the autumn fruits to be safely stored against the winter's need, and encouraged man to continue in one spot, building himself a stable house and tilling the soil, was no doubt one of the prime causes of human development. It is as a powerful contribution to, if not as an essential condition of human development, that private property is rightly regarded as "natural."

There are three chief grounds given in the Christian tradition for this view that private property is, if not part of the natural law, at the least a wholesome supplement to it. The first is concerned with what we nowadays call "incentives." Whether as a result of the Fall or not it is by the sweat of his brow that man lives. There is a great deal of hard unpleasant and uninteresting work to be done, if man is to clothe and feed and house himself and his family: still more if he is to amass such a store of wealth as to have leisure for the development of the arts and sciences, and be able both to tend the sick and aged, and in general to support all the members of a society in a condition free from desperate want. Private property, whereby a man enjoys of right the fruits of his own labours, provides the essential stimulus and incentive to work. The wealth amassed by that hard labour redounds inevitably in some degree to the good of the whole society; whether it so redounds to the greatest degree possible depends on the social morality of its members; but that it redounds in some degree is certain. For if no one works or no one works hard, the whole community is impoverished. The first reason for private property then, is that by the incentive which it provides for industry it benefits the common good.

The second reason for private property is that it fosters the division of labour and so increases efficiency. The right to enjoy the fruit of one's labour incites men to labour at that which brings them the greatest reward. Accordingly everybody chooses what he can do best and turn most to his own advantage, and strives to increase his skill and aptitude for that particular thing. This in turn increases the general efficiency of labour and so redounds to the advantage of the community.

The third reason is that private property prevents a great deal of squabbling and discontent. This seems an odd statement, because we are accustomed to think that private property, with its discrepancy between rich and poor, is precisely the chief cause of envy and discontent. But the tradition presupposes that the ownership of material things bears some rough proportion to the degree and quality of the labour which each man contributes, and contrasts with such a condition the inevitable alternative. If there is no private property, if all material things are commonly owned, there must be some kind of distribution of them to the individuals to satisfy their present needs. This distribution could be effected by physical force—first come first served, and the devil take the hindmost. There could be no more effective method of disrupting society, impoverishing the community and filling the lives of individuals with strife and discontent. Alternatively, the distribution could be made by authority. If the distribution so made were precisely equal, a wide door would be open to the complaints of those who have special needs or who have made an especially valuable contribution. If the distribution were made according to need and merit, opportunity is given for endless disputes and complaints that individuals' needs and merits have been wrongly assessed.

On the whole, human nature being what it is, the fairest distribution is ensured by the institution of private property which gives to each man the right to own the fruits of his own labour. It allows him to have and to enjoy both that which he earns and that which he receives from others by inheritance, gift or exchange. And being the fairest, it promotes best the peace and harmony of society.

These three grounds envisage private property as a social institution, and defend it as essential to the welfare of society. An even stronger defence, as I think, is to be found in the necessity of private property for the development of the individual. The divine purpose for each one of us is that we grow into a fully developed and integrated person. We become persons through the exercise of our power of choice, by our freedom to select the conscious ends we pursue, and adapt the means at our disposal to attain them. We grow by reflection upon past experience, and by using that experience in making our choices for the present and the future. It is essential that every man have material upon which to exercise this power of choice. Hence the right to personal freedom, and the right to choose one's work. Hence, above all, the right to freedom of worship and conscience, the right, that is, to worship in the truth as we apprehend it, and the right to do our duty as we conceive it. But the most obvious sphere of choice lies in the management of the material things which constitute our immediate environment.

The first sign in children of their being "grown up" is an insistent demand for money of their own: they want money so that they may be able to choose and buy their own clothes, to decide for themselves whether to go or not to go to the theatre or pictures, to choose their own holiday place, in fact to make all the different choices which the possession of money of their own puts in their power. This is right and natural, for it is by making choices of this kind that their own personalities are developed. And this is the function of private property. It is the means whereby we can control in some measure our environment. It affords us the power to decide for ourselves whether to be thrifty or prodigal, mean or generous, to pursue this interest or that. And by these decisions our characters are formed.

Though the wider the range the greater the power of choice, the essential requirement of private property is satisfied if each individual has the ownership of his food and clothes, and nothing more. The slave, though severely limited and handicapped, has yet the capacity to become a person, not only because he holds it in his power to make moral choices—for example, to give generous or grudging service, to help or injure his fellow-slaves—but because he has power over some material things, at least in the matter of their disposal. Yet there is another function of private property which demands its more extensive possession. Private property is a bulwark of freedom. This is the inner meaning of the phrase "an Englishman's home is his castle." A man with no property is defenceless against misfortune. He is overwhelmed by sudden catastrophes and driven to courses of action which he would not freely choose. A man with no property is at the mercy of his superiors. He must do what they tell him or starve. The ownership of property, the possession of savings, enables a man to resign an occupation which he finds is driving him to wrongful action, and gives him time to look around for other work. In this way the possession of private property supports and protects individual freedom. The more highly organized and centralized a community is and the more monopolistic its industries, the more important it is that the independence which private property gives should be as widely distributed as possible. In no other way can the individual be free against the pressure of his fellows, nor minorities maintain their existence.

Ownership implies complete possession, the right to do with a thing what one likes—to use it, give it away, sell it, or destroy it. But the absolute right of ownership is of course subject to the moral law, which imposes considerable restrictions on our use of our property. The first and most extensive restriction is that private property must always be used so as to serve, directly or indirectly, the common good. This is because man owns nothing in his own right, but only in trust for God the Creator. God creates material things through nature for the common use of the human species in general, and accordingly individual owners must use those things for the common good. So a man in absolutely desperate need is justified in taking so much of another's property as will satisfy his immediate need, even though the owner has refused his request. For the owner's refusal was wrong and unreasonable.

In the same way, where the interest of the community imperatively demands that property be used in a certain way, the community is justified in enforcing such use by positive law, in spite of the owner's refusal. This is the moral justification of the practice of commandeering property in wartime, and of the peacetime compulsory acquisition of neglected or ill-farmed land, the taking over of inefficiently run industries, the requisitioning of land urgently required for building purposes and other similar measures. The Christian defence of private property does not contest the rightness of such actions in the interest of the common good : it only insists that for them to be right the common good must really need such restrictions of the rights of property, and that the interest of the community must not be allowed wholly to destroy the rights of the individual. It is for this reason that fair compensation is always due.

The absolute right of an owner to do what he likes with his property is further restricted by the duty to respect the rights of others. I may not use my property in such a way that it becomes a source of injury to my neighbour. For example, I have a right to burn my field of stubble, if I want to. But I may not use that right if the wind is going to carry the flames on to my neighbour's field of standing corn. I have a right to cut down one of my trees, if I want to ; but not in such a way as to cause it to fall on my neighbour's roof. It is this duty to respect the rights of others which underlies the many laws in restraint of public nuisances. The idea is so familiar to us that it needs no further comment. Justice demands that we so exercise our own rights as not to violate the clear rights of our neighbours. In certain cases positive law supports and supplements the moral law by ordering forcible and physical restraint, and by inflicting punishment on those who violate the rights of others. This is done for the sake of the peace of society.

However, all that positive law does not forbid and that conscience does not in addition condemn is within the rights of the individual. Subject to those limitations he may use his possessions as he wills. And, so far as is compatible with the peace and general well-being of society, the widest possible latitude of choice is desirable. It is better for a man— it is the divine method—that he should be free to choose between good and bad, even at the risk of choosing bad. When positive law by compulsory legislation enforces a right use of property and dictates in detail how a man shall employ what is his own, to that extent it dictates to conscience and narrows the area of moral choice which it is one of the functions of private property to enlarge. Such legislation may produce a well-organized society with a high average standard of living; it will not help to produce developed human persons. Persons develop by the exercise of free choice, and the ownership of property provides especial scope for this, by requiring persons to decide how they will use that property, what are the claims of others upon them in justice and charity and what is the extent to which they are morally entitled to spend their money on themselves.

The right use of property demands that it shall contribute directly or indirectly to the common good. To hoard money for the mere pleasure of possessing it is the self-indulgent vice of the miser. To own more than one can enjoy oneself and not to use the surplus to promote the common good is meanness. To use the right to enjoy one's wealth in disregard of the crying need of others is hardness. All property is, in a sense, a trust, to be wisely and discreetly used. Its possession imposes grave responsibilities. Yet the requirement that all property serve the common good directly or indirectly is capable of a very wide interpretation and in no way rules out all expenditure on personal needs and pleasures.

It does not, for example, forbid but rather enjoins a wise expenditure on the education of a man's children and the placing of them in the world. It enjoins a wise provision for old age and the old age of our dependents. Nor does it forbid the creation of pleasant surroundings and amenities in which a man, his family and his friends may live. A beautiful house and garden, good furniture, books and pictures, and a family in appreciative and satisfied enjoyment of them are an asset to society: a multiplication of them is the enrichment of society. Nor is all expenditure on amusement and recreations illegitimate. For in so far as these are necessary to health, efficiency and happiness, by making any one man healthy, happy and efficient such expenditure so far contributes to the common good. Once more to repeat the point: the moral value and justification of private property is that its possession forces men to decide how to use it, and so provides the material for the formation of character. At the same time it constitutes a bulwark of independence and in that way also increases moral freedom. The good of society therefore requires the greatest possible number of owners of property, and the least possible interference in the use of it.

There are three main ways in which property is distributed in a society: that is to say, there are three main ways of acquiring property. The first way is by gift or inheritance. An owner may give all or some of his property to another person. Provided the recipient accepts the gift, and provided the donor is the true owner of the property, the right of ownership passes irrevocably to the recipient. If I give half-a-crown to a beggar, the moment I have given it and he has taken it, the half-a-crown becomes his, and I cannot claim it back. Inheritance is a kind of acquisition by gift. For a will is the written statement of the owner's desire for the disposition of his property at his death. In it he expresses his will that it be given to such and such persons. Where no will is made, society confers the ownership on the next of kin; partly because the property can be regarded as in a sense the property not only of the individual owner but of his family whose maintenance is a first charge on it, and who are therefore entitled to it; and partly because society judges that the owner of it ought to have and would have given it to his next of kin. In any case, the justification of a title to property by inheritance is that it is in fact a gift from the dead owner.

The second method of acquiring property is by labour. The things which a man makes or which are the result of his labour are his. To this, however, there is a qualification. They are only his if the materials out of which he makes them are his. Thus the crops which a farmer grows are his, and so is the furniture which a carpenter makes. The workers in a factory do not own the things produced in the factory, because the machinery and the materials are not theirs. Whether by reason of the labour which they have contributed they have a rightful claim to part ownership of the products of the factory is a difficult and disputed question.

On the one hand it may reasonably be held that labour is equally essential to production with management and capital, and is therefore entitled to a joint-ownership of what is jointly produced. On the other hand it may be retorted that by accepting a fixed wage labour has sold its services and forfeited any claim it may have to ownership of the things produced. If it is going to claim any such ownership, it must forgo wages and be content with its share in the worth of the things produced, whatever that may turn out to be. It is not easy to see where justice lies. The older view undoubtedly has been that the wage-earner has no claim to any share of the ownership of the things which he produces out of the materials supplied by others. He is justly rewarded for his labour by the wages for which he has contracted to sell his labour.

In a predominantly agricultural and small-manufacturing economy, this is a not intolerable judgement. In the economy of large industrialized communities, however, it results in an unhealthy restriction of the ownership of private property, and the view is rapidly gaining ground that justice demands that all who contribute to production should have, over and above their wages, some share in the ownership of the things produced, proportionate to the value of their contribution. Hence the emergence of profit-sharing, co-partnership and joint-ownership schemes. There can be no doubt that, in so far as they give added dignity to the status of wage-earners, and increase in them an interest and pride in their work, and also in so far as they re-inforce the understanding that by their labour men serve both the community and themselves, such schemes are in accordance with the teaching of Christian ethics about the place and duty of the individual in society.

The third, and most usual, way of acquiring property is by a contract of exchange. The simplest form of this is barter. "As every schoolboy knows," it is possible to obtain possession of a coveted stamp by means of a "swop." The object of this transaction is to enable each of the two parties to it to obtain something which they want, by surrendering something for which they have no use, or which they want less. As a result of the transaction both parties are pleased and satisfied. It is to facilitate such agreements that money exists. It generally happens that the owner of the thing which I covet does not desire the object which I am prepared to surrender in exchange for it : he does, however, desire something in the possession of a third person, or a number of things in the possession of several different persons. Accordingly he accepts from me a sum of money, as a token of value, which the other persons are prepared in their turn to accept from him, and so on. In this way a series of exchanges of property takes place and money is "the medium of exchange." The amount of money which a man will happily accept in return for surrendering something which he possesses is that amount by means of which he can obtain for himself possession of some other thing or things which he wants more than the thing which he already has. In other words money exists in order to facilitate an equality of exchange, and its proper use is the "just price."

From at least the time of St. Thomas Aquinas onwards the idea of the just price has dominated Christian teaching on economic matters. The just price is the price which gives to each of the parties to the contract a roughly equal benefit. What precisely that price is depends on a delicate appreciation of the particular circumstances of each case. It cannot be stated in general terms. For practical purposes it is sometimes officially laid down by the state, sometimes fixed by the general agreement of traders—the market price—sometimes, where some unusual circumstances are present, by a particular agreement between the two parties. The important thing is that Christian ethics stresses the duty of everyone to aim at and be content with the just price, and not to strive for something more. And the just price is that of which an impartial observer may say that both parties ought to be satisfied. Equal advantage, mutual satisfaction and common benefit are the goal at which all who are engaged in commercial deals must aim.

Accordingly Christian ethics holds it to be illegitimate to try and sell your goods for more than they are worth. It expressly forbids you to make a profit out of your neighbour's need or ignorance. It explicitly condemns the maxim "seek to buy in the cheapest and sell in the dearest market" as a true or safe guide to commercial conduct. The particular application of the just price principle is, of course, complex and difficult. To discuss the exceptions and modifications which have to be introduced would involve us in a lengthy casuistic digression for which this is not the time or place. There is no easy rule of thumb for arriving at the just price or determining the worth of any article in all sets of circumstances. Thus to the rule that one must not sell things for more than they are worth, an exception has to be made in the case of merchants and shop-keepers, to allow of a reasonable profit in return for the service they render as providers and purveyors of merchandise. Or again something may justly be added to the ordinary price when the owner is reluctant to sell and only agrees as a favour to the purchaser.

Perhaps the easiest way of conveying Christian teaching on these matters is to give one or two examples. Thus, Baxter answers the question "May I desire or take more than my labour or goods are worth ?" in this way. "Not by deceit, persuading another that they are worth more than they are. Not by extortion working on men's ignorance, error or necessity. Not of any one that is poorer than yourself. But if you deal with the rich, who in generosity or liberality stick not at a small matter and are willing another should be a gainer by them, and understand what they do, it is lawful to take as much as they will give you." Or again, to the question "May I buy as cheap as I can get it or give less than the thing is worth ?" he replies, "If it be worth more to you than the market price (through your necessity) you are not bound to give above the market price : if it be worth less to you than the market price you are not bound to give more than it is worth to you, as suited to your use. But you must not desire to seek to get another's goods or labour for less than it is worth in both respects (in common estimate, and to you)." "May I take advantage of another's ignorance or error in bargaining ?" "Not to get more than your commodity is worth, nor to get his goods for less than the worth." And finally, Baxter ends this section on "Special cases about justice in buying and selling" with the words : "Love your neighbours as yourselves : Do as you would be done by : and oppress not your poor brethren ; and then by these three rules you will yourselves decide a multitude of such doubts and difficulties." (*Christian Directory*.)

It is certain that attention to those three rules, which are the underlying principle of Christian business ethics, would ensure a more just and equitable distribution of property, go far to remove hatred, bitterness and suspicion between employers and employed, result in fair wages and fair labour in return for them, and in general make the whole business of production and distribution an honourable means of service to the community. For Christian ethics teaches both that a man is fairly entitled to a reward for his labour, and also that his labour must be worthy of the reward.

Property is justly acquired by gift, by the sale of services, by the exchange one already has, or by the fruits of one's labour. But both the acquisition and the enjoyment of property are to be governed by the claims of justice and of charity. A man may take no more than his due, he must use it so as not to injure his neighbour, and he must in charity consider the needs of others.

There is one particular kind of contract by which property is acquired which is so much a matter of debate and controversy to-day that it requires longer consideration in a chapter to itself. That is the gambling contract.

CHAPTER VI

GAMBLING

A GAMBLING contract is an agreement between two or more persons whereby they mutually covenant that a particular sum of money shall be paid to one or more of them in accordance with the issue of a particular event. The result is that, as the event turns out, some pay and some receive. Although the Christian tradition has never condemned such contracts as being intrinsically and necessarily vicious, they have been looked upon with grave suspicion and individuals have from time to time denounced them as inherently wrong.

The grounds upon which all gambling is condemned are two: first that it makes the exchange of property depend merely on chance, and secondly that it is an attempt to get something for nothing. It is held that material things may rightly change hands as a result of a gift—in accordance with friendship, gratitude or need—or as a result of labour, as a just reward of industry, or as a result of an exchange, when one thing is surrendered in return for another. But it is wrong to make the possession of material things depend merely on chance.

It is not easy to see at once the force of this argument. Many things depend on chance, in the sense that they depend on an uncertain future event, an event of which we have no present certain knowledge whether it will turn out this way or that. In agriculture much depends on the incalculable weather. In deciding whether to send one's children to boarding school or to keep them at home, there are many uncertain unpredictable factors involved, which if we could but have certain knowledge of them, would influence our decision this way or that. In most decisions, and often the most important, much has to be left to chance in the sense of the unknown or uncertain. And more than that, circumstances sometimes arise in which the only possible procedure is by an appeal to chance. I can think of no other way of deciding which of two teams shall bat first in a cricket match or kick off at football. Where two or more persons have an equal claim to something which they cannot both have and which cannot be shared between them, the only fair solution is an appeal to chance in which they are both on an equality. How else should the possession, say, of a picture be determined between claimants with an exactly equal claim?

Still, it might be replied, one ought to try first to settle these things on a reasonable basis. In most cases claims are not equally justified. Enquiry and consideration will show an advantage on one side or another. The wrong in gambling is that it ignores all claims of need or merit and makes the ownership of material things depend merely and unnecessarily on chance. This is an offence against reason. We hold material things in trust, to use them properly for the sustenance of ourselves and our family, for profitable employment to the enrichment of the common wealth, and for the relief and betterment of our neighbours. We have no right, it is a misuse of them, to risk their loss unnecessarily, and we have no right to try and acquire more of them simply by an appeal to chance.

This form of the argument, that gambling involves an unnecessary and so unreasonable appeal to chance, is more convincing. Yet it is not strong enough to warrant a condemnation of all gambling as such. It is clear that it is unreasonable and wrong to risk the loss unnecessarily of all or of a substantial part of our possessions. Those possessions exist as a buttress and support of our individual freedom, and as providing scope for the development of our personalities: they are a protection against unpredictable misfortune. Unnecessarily to risk their loss is to go directly counter to the very reason for their existence. It is clearly wrong. That is why excessive gambling—gambling with the baby's milk—is wholly without any justification. But there is a very great deal of gambling which falls far short of this, and involves the risk of losing only a small portion of our possession. It is not clear that this must necessarily be wrong.

Indeed there is one class of transaction in which we think it to be self-evidently right—insurance. When I insure my house against fire I risk the total loss of my premium year by year. I make a bet with the insurance company. If there is a fire they pay me a considerable sum, if there is no fire I pay them the premium. The possession of material things is thus made wholly dependent on an uncertain event—fire or no fire. And we think this entirely right. Therefore to risk the loss of a part of our possessions, to make its ownership dependent on an uncertain event, cannot of itself be wrong. If gambling is intrinsically wrong, it must be for some other reason than this.

But, it is said, we ought not to try and acquire possessions simply through an appeal to chance. That is trying to get something for nothing. Possessions ought to be distributed in accordance with need or merit. We must either receive them as a spontaneous unconditional gift, or we must earn them. We must not beg for them, or try and get them without doing anything in return for them. We may, of course, receive them also as a conditional gift—conditional on our making a particular use of them, or of our acceding to some prior request on the part of the donor. But such conditional gifts are reducible either to unconditional gifts if the condition is not enforced, or to a form of earning or exchange if our possession is obtained strictly in return for the fulfilment of the fixed conditions.

There are, I think, two possible answers to the argument that gambling is an attempt to get something for nothing and therefore in principle wrong. The first answer is that to get something for nothing in the form of a gift is not in principle wrong, and that the winnings in a gamble may properly be regarded as a gift. A gamble is a bargain that one person will give to another a part of his possessions if a particular uncertain event turns out in a particular way. It is a conditional gift. It would only be wrong if what the loser covenants to give is not his to give ; if, that is, he either has no money of his own, or what he has is already and wholly needed for other purposes. This, again, only proves that gambling with stakes greater than one can afford to lose is wrong. It says nothing against gambling well within one's means.

However, a stronger because truer argument is to deny that gambling is an attempt to get something for nothing. In every gamble all the parties involved confer a right on each other in certain circumstances to claim a payment. Each party buys that contingent right to claim, when he stakes his money. A right to claim payment is not nothing. The loser in a gamble does not make the winner a free gift. It was conditional on the winner having pledged himself in the event of certain circumstances to admit a similar claim on the part of the loser. The winner receives his winnings as a result of having exposed himself to the risk of being the loser and having to pay. He gave in return for his winnings and as the condition of his receiving them this potential right.

It is, of course, quite true that in the event the loser's right turns out to be valueless. In that sense the winner gets his winnings for nothing. But if the winner gains all as the result of the gamble and the loser receives no money, it does not follow that the loser has received nothing at all. It is worth while looking at the practice of insurance again. When I insure my house against fire for a year, if there is no fire the insurance company wins my premium and gives me nothing in return. There could scarcely be a clearer instance of "something for nothing." The insurance company would of course reply indignantly that it was nothing of the sort. For a whole year they have exposed themselves to the risk of being obliged to pay out a very considerable sum of money, in return for the relatively worthless premium which they received. It is precisely the successful gambler's answer—he ran the risk of losing, he put himself in a position where he might have been obliged to pay out. Still, it might be replied, whatever risk the insurance company ran, in the end they got my premium for nothing. But did they? If that were really so, people would not be so eager to insure. In fact, the insurance company did me a very great service in return for my premium. They freed me from all anxiety about the loss of my property through fire. It was that freedom from anxiety which I bought with my premium, and which was my reason for insuring. And providing that freedom from anxiety is the chief business of an insurance company and the justification for its existence.

It might be said at this point that that is just the difference between insurance and gambling, and why a comparison between the two is unfair and misleading. Insurance companies perform a social service. They benefit the community by providing a means of spreading risk, and so freeing the individual from the tyranny of sudden catastrophic misfortune. By means of insurance companies a loss which would be too great a burden for any individual to bear, is distributed over a wider whole. In gambling there is no such service. But is that so? Once you set off against a material loss, an immaterial intangible benefit it becomes clear that the argument that gambling must be wrong because it is an attempt to get something for nothing has to be abandoned. Gambling is not an attempt to get something for nothing. It is, in a way, the opposite of insurance.

In insurance, to repeat it once more, the company gets the premium, the customer gets freedom from anxiety. Both parties are satisfied, and so far as is possible an equitable exchange has been effected between a sum of money and a state of mind. It is of course out of the question to balance these incommensurables exactly, but a rough equilibrium is found where a great number of people are willing to pay a particular premium. That means that they judge that their freedom from anxiety is roughly worth that amount. In gambling the loser buys with his stake not freedom from anxiety but the precise opposite, uncertain expectation. He buys a state of mind in which he alternates between pleasurable expectation of gain and nervous apprehension of loss. Just as in insurance men club together to pool their losses and thereby enjoy immunity from the fear of loss, just as they agree that all shall contribute something to the payment of the losses of the few; so in gambling men club together for exactly the opposite purpose. The parties to a gambling contract agree that all shall contribute to the winnings of a few and thereby all shall enjoy expectation of gain. This is particularly clear in the case of sweepstakes and football pools. These are agreements that someone shall have a prize which individually is beyond the reach of any of them. To this end they club together and ensure that by thus pooling some or all of their surplus wealth one at least of them shall certainly be possessed of a sum which none of them otherwise could ever hope to secure.

I do not think that it can in itself be any more wrong to receive £30,000 from an insurance company, which one has done nothing to earn or deserve beyond the payment of a totally disproportionate premium, than it is to receive £30,000 from the organizers of a football pool in return for a similarly disproportionate stake. It is sometimes said in reply to this argument that the man who receives compensation from the insurance company for the loss of his house by fire, is no better off than he was before the fire, and so cannot be said to have gained anything. This is true, but irrelevant. He is very much better off than he would have been after the fire if he had not insured. In return for the payment of a small premium he finds himself in possession of the value of a house which no longer exists. In both gambling and insurance one side obtains a tangible reward for which it has given to the other side nothing—or nothing proportionate—in return. In both cases, a public service is rendered. Insurance companies purvey a sense of security : gambling promoters purvey a particular kind of pleasure.

We have, I think, reached the position in which it is clear that if gambling is wrong in itself, it is not because of the appeal to chance, or because it gets something for nothing, but because it deliberately fosters and promotes a particular state of mind ; because it produces a particular kind of pleasurable excitement closely associated with the desire for gain, and has no other purpose except the promotion of this excitement. If gambling is wrong it is because this pleasurable excitement is itself wrong.

This, I am sure, is the root of the matter. Many people, whose moral judgements in other matters command the deepest respect, are convinced that while to desire compensation for undeserved calamitous loss and so freedom from anxiety is rational and right, to desire undeserved and unearned riches, and to put oneself in a position of unsettling anticipation is irrational and wrong. In other words, they think that it is necessarily immoral to buy the hope of gain. Unless they adduce reasons for this opinion, it is of course impossible to take the matter further. You either agree or disagree. In so far as reasons are adduced, they must, I imagine, take some such form as this. The hope of gain, thus unrelated to any effort or industry by which the gain may be earned and deserved, necessarily induces a false conception of the nature and purpose of wealth. It forcibly suggests that wealth exists for private enjoyment, not for public service. It divorces wealth from the idea of responsibility, as being the reward of service and the means of service. Secondly the hope of undeserved gains breeds discontent with our present condition and at the same time undermines our resolution to improve that condition by our own industry. Thirdly, the pleasurable excitement associated with the hope of gain breeds avarice, it fosters an excessive and disproportionate concentration on the acquisition of wealth to the detriment of other and more important interests in life.

That these are very often the effects of gambling cannot be denied. What is not clear is that they are the necessary effects of all gambling. To hope for a large prize in a football pool does not seem to be essentially different from hoping to inherit a large estate from an uncle. It is not clear why unearned wealth should forcibly suggest a false conception of the purpose of wealth. It might with equal cogency be argued that where all private property is exclusively the reward of individual merit and industry there arises a strong suggestion that wealth is a personal reward, that what has already been earned by public service, public service has no further claims upon.

In other words, it might well be maintained that it is precisely unearned wealth which induces and fosters a sense of responsibility. For it demands an answer to the question "Why am I thus favoured?" a question which is never even posed to the man who knows that he has earned his wealth by his own energy and ability. Moreover, there are many instances of successful gamblers exercising the greatest sense of responsibility in the administration of their new-found wealth. Secondly, the hope of gain does not inevitably breed discontent. To argue so is to condemn all hope as immoral. The hope of heaven does not breed discontent with life on earth, but stimulates the resolution to make the best use of it. Similarly, the hope of gain and of improving or altering our standard of living does not necessarily breed discontent and undermine industry. It may stimulate industry by increasing a proper reluctance to acquiesce indefinitely in unnecessary discomfort. Thirdly, the existence of huge numbers of moderate gamblers in whose lives gambling occupies a minor position among recreative amusements disposes of the argument that gambling must necessarily lead to avarice and inevitably become an obsession.

It is always distasteful to argue against the deep moral convictions of persons for whom one has a natural respect. What has so far been said is not intended to do more than suggest that the conviction that gambling must necessarily be wrong is not self-evidently true, and to show that the arguments by which that conviction is generally supported do not, in fact, amount to more than a proof, if proof were needed, that gambling is often excessive, and that such excessive gambling is necessarily wrong. It now remains to attempt something more positive, to establish the proper nature of gambling considered in itself and the limitations within which it may be regarded as a legitimate activity.

It seems that gambling is properly to be regarded as a recreative amusement. It is under that category if any that it occupies a legitimate position. The kind of recreative amusement which it is may be most clearly seen if we start by considering games of chance. When people sit down to play bridge or poker or even dice, their proper object is the recreation which those games provide. That recreation consists in taking their minds off their ordinary work and worries, and resting them by giving them another occupation. The interest and excitement of the game keeps their minds on the game and off their work and worries. Often, however, the game is insufficiently interesting to distract from the worry, and it is a general experience that the interest and excitement of the game can be greatly increased if the people agree that the winners shall receive a sum of money from the losers. The expectation of gain and the apprehension of loss ensure that the game is played with keenness and concentration. In this way the maximum of relaxation and recreation is obtained.

Now it is essential that the gambling element should be subordinate to the recreational. In other words it is essential that the players play primarily for the sake of the game and only secondarily for the sake of winning whatever stakes there are. Otherwise, if the gambling element predominates, the game ceases to be a game and so recreative; it becomes a business and, so far from relaxing the mind and freeing it from anxiety and worry, increases worry. The game then defeats its own end. Such gambling is therefore wrong. We thus arrive at the proper limit of legitimate gambling, at least so far as games of chance are concerned. So long as the gambling stimulates the interest and keenness with which the game is played, it is recreative and legitimate. When it passes beyond that stage, so that the interest passes from the game and is wholly concentrated on the fear of loss or hope of gain, then it defeats its own object, is the opposite of recreative, and is wrong.

The same considerations apply to betting on horse-racing, at least in the case of those who bet on the course itself as part of the amusement of watching the races. The proper object of such betting is to increase the interest and excitement of the races, and thereby the concentration and pleasure with which we watch them. In this way we are "taken completely out of ourselves" and obtain from this "outing" the fullest recreational value. But, to be legitimate, the gambling must be subordinate to the races.

In other words, there are certain forms of gambling which clearly serve the subordinate purpose of enhancing and increasing the recreational value of the activities to which they are attached; and to that extent they are certainly innocent. Where, however, those activities are treated merely as an excuse or occasion for gambling, these kinds of gambling may be judged to be excessive. Certainly they change their character and become instances of another form of gambling of which the recreational value consists solely in the pleasurable excitement of anticipation. This form of gambling, in which gambling is, so to speak, an end in itself, is perhaps the most popular and widely-practised, as is shown by the modern prevalence of lotteries, sweepstakes and football pools. The question which it poses is that of the value and legitimacy of this particular kind of pleasure.

Considered in itself, this state of pleasurable anticipation, which such gambling is designed to create, is analogous to the child's eager anticipation of a birthday or Christmas. There does not seem to be anything intrinsically vicious about such excitement. Indeed, to have something pleasant to look forward to may provide a valuable mental tonic. It has the effect of stimulus. In filling in his football coupon or buying a ticket in a sweepstake a man is purchasing this particular form of amusement. It is a kind of "outing." It gives him something to think about and promotes pleasurable sensations. Yet here again, the practice defeats its own end if the gambling becomes predominant, so that a man's chief preoccupation and concern centres round his expectation of winning. So far from being a recreative amusement, gambling then becomes a source of unsettlement and displaces from their proper position those interests and activities which ought to take first place in a man's thoughts and work.

The conclusion so far reached is this. Gambling, within certain limits, is a legitimate method of amusement and recreation. The popular opinion is endorsed that there is nothing wrong in an occasional shilling on a horse or in playing bridge for moderate stakes, or in filling in a weekly football coupon. It is a form of amusement which does not, perhaps, rank very high in the cultural scale. It has markedly less recreative value than art, literature, gardening or ball games. Yet for all that, within its own limits it has some recreative value, and therefore a man may legitimately include it among his amusements if he wants to. What he may not legitimately do is to convert it from being an amusement into being a business.

He may not gamble to excess. He should at all times bear in mind that his amusements and recreations should never consume more than a small proportion of his time, energy and income. They stand to his life as a whole, as a sauce stands to the dish which it seasons. As it is greedy and ridiculous to have a vast quantity of jam on a minute fragment of bread (for then nourishment, the purpose of eating, is frustrated, being subordinated to the pleasure of taste; whereas the pleasure of taste exists to promote eating and so nourishment) so it is dissipated and ridiculous to spend the bulk of our time and energy on amusement and only a small fraction on our serious occupations. Because amusements are only justified as providing a stimulus to enable us to do our proper work better. Two things have to be borne in mind. First, that it is unwise and untrue to forbid people to spend anything on amusements. And secondly, that it is unreasonable and self-indulgent for people to spend too much on amusements.

The Christian church has never condemned gambling as intrinsically evil, but has at all times allowed it a place among legitimate amusements. But there is no doubt that it has allowed that place grudgingly, because, perhaps more than any other amusement, gambling lends itself to abuse and excess. And more than excessive indulgence in any other amusement, excessive gambling has disastrous effects upon character. If a man gives up all his time and thought and money to playing golf, he probably becomes a bore and certainly does not do his duty in making a proper contribution to the common wealth, but his general character does not necessarily deteriorate. For an exclusive interest in golf, though narrow, is not corruptive. Again, a man who goes disproportionately often to the cinema is no doubt idle and vacant. But unless he chooses particularly low films to patronize, he will not become worse than an idler. With gambling it is otherwise. The pleasure of golf and the passive entertainment of the cinema are of such a kind that an excess of them is merely excessive. Its effect on character is negative —it engenders waste of time and omission of positive duty.

An excess of gambling, on the other hand, has positive effects. The proper pleasure in gambling comes so close to greed and avarice that even a little too much of it turns it into avarice. The nervous apprehension of loss which is a necessary element in the recreative pleasure of gambling can so easily turn into anxiety and fear and produce a restless malaise. Thus the effects of excessive gambling on character are disastrous and are very quick to show themselves. They are an insatiable desire for easy money and a consequent reluctance to work, and a feverish absorption in anticipation and speculation to the exclusion of all other interests. When this practice, which should add a small element of pleasurable excitement, is allowed to become the main ingredient it inevitably creates an unstable and restless character, whose only permanent quality is a hard selfish greed.

Excessive gambling leads to a rapid moral deterioration, distinguished by a selfish indifference to the needs of others, continuous inability to work or to concentrate on anything beside the issues of successive gambles, and a general restless instability. Moreover, the temptation to greed implicit in all gambling is so insidious and strong that the transition from moderate legitimate recreative gambling to excessive immoral and destructive gambling is fatally easy. And once that transition is made it is correspondingly difficult to retrace one's steps.

It is because the amusement of gambling is thus dangerous that the Christian tradition has always frowned upon it, and in various ways discouraged it. And the evils of gambling may at certain times be so great and widespread that it becomes the duty of a Christian to abstain from it altogether. It is the commonly accepted view that such a condition obtains in England to-day. It is difficult to be sure whether and how far there is in fact excessive gambling. The publication of figures showing the gross takings of totalisators and football pools do not of themselves prove its existence. They are not probably much greater than the takings of the cinema industry, and they do not prove that the average adult is either spending too great a proportion of his income in this way or allowing it to occupy a disproportionate amount of his time and mental energy.

It is, at least, conceivable that by far the greater number of those who take part in football pools waste no more time and money on them than others spend on going to the cinema, and obtain from them greater recreation and refreshment. However, it is the general testimony of those who are in the best position to know that all over England there is evidence of widespread excessive gambling. It is said to show itself in restless feverish excitement, in inability for steady work, in discontent, and in poverty. Its results are to be seen in a neglect of family and social responsibilities and in a general increase in dishonesty and crime.

This excessive gambling is alleged to be most prevalent, as we should expect, in industrial and urban areas. For it is precisely the drab environment and mechanical labour which make up the lives of those who live in such areas which most imperatively demand the kind of amusement and excitement which gambling provides. And the amount of gambling is not likely to decrease appreciably until on the one hand a higher general level of education opens up more fruitful and recreative ways of occupying leisure, and on the other an increased understanding of the place of their own particular labour in the general scheme of things and an increased share in the management and control of the actual conditions of their labour, reduce the elements of drudgery and monotony. Meanwhile the existence of such widespread excessive gambling with its baleful results in moral deterioration confronts the Christian, and indeed everyone, with an ethical problem.

"All things are lawful, but all things are not expedient." It may be perfectly legitimate for anyone to gamble, within the limits which I have tried to describe, and yet it may be his duty not to gamble. This duty would derive from the duty to love our neighbour. In other words, a general obligation to abstain from gambling might be based not on the ground that all gambling is essentially wrong—that would be a duty owed in justice—but on the ground that it harms other people—a duty of charity. There are many warnings in the Bible against making other people stumble, against being a cause of offence to them. The meaning of these warnings is that it is a primary obligation of neighbourly love, of social good behaviour, not to tempt others to do what is wrong. It is not only by direct and deliberate incitement that we can tempt others. Any flagrant bad example constitutes a temptation to others, and we are guilty of making others offend although we had no such desire or intention. A man is responsible for the normal inevitable consequences of his actions, whether he consciously wills them or not. But not only are we guilty in this way when we set a bad example by publicly and flagrantly doing what is wrong, we may also tempt others when what we do is perfectly legitimate and harmless.

Gambling provides a very good example of this. If it be true that a very great number of our neighbours are in the grip of the gambling fever, if they are spending on this amusement more than they can or should afford and if this amusement is corrupting their character, it becomes an imperative duty for us not to do anything which can in any way encourage them or make it easier for them to go on gambling. Now whilst it is no doubt true that demand creates supply, it is also true that supply fosters and creates demand. The desire to gamble will always find ways and means of satisfying itself; but, equally, ready-to-hand facilities for gambling will increase the demand. A man who becomes aware that he is in danger of gambling too much may be able to resist the temptation if he has to search about to find the means of gambling. Conversely, many a man may slide into excessive gambling by thoughtlessly making use continuously of the facilities for gambling which are so constantly presented to him. The vast business of organized gambling is undoubtedly the cause as well as the effect of the present nation-wide indulgence in gambling.

If, then, gambling is excessive it appears to be an obvious duty not to increase these facilities. Not because being a bookmaker or running a football pool is in itself immoral—it may be just as legitimate a way of catering for public amusement as running a cinema—but because the more facilities there are of this kind, the more people are encouraged to gamble excessively. And whether we intend it or not, by our action to encourage people or to make it easier for them to gamble too much is to share ourselves in their sin.

Further, it seems that not only would it be wrong to

start, say, a football pool; it would also be wrong to take part in one. Everybody who makes use of the existing gambling facilities, even though there is nothing wrong in itself in what he does, contributes to the support of these facilities. Clearly, if there were a widespread boycott of them, many of the firms would go out of business. And that would be no bad thing. Every time I take part in organized gambling I am, to that extent, directly maintaining in existence the instrument and means of my neighbour's moral deterioration. His guilt lies partially at my door.

Accordingly, it would appear that where there is widespread excessive gambling it becomes the duty of the Christian to abstain from all forms of public organized gambling and to confine his amusement of this sort to those occasions and circumstances when he is quite certain that what he does will not directly or indirectly be a source of temptation to others. This raises the question of whether it is legitimate to organize "raffles" as a means of raising money at Church bazaars and such-like occasions. There are many who hold that quite apart from the rightness or wrongness of gambling considered in itself, for the Church to countenance it officially by allowing such methods of raising money to be employed is to set a bad example and to fail in her pastoral duty. People always try to salve their own conscience by pointing to the example of others. They are very ready to infer that because a thing is sometimes right in some circumstances, it is always right in all circumstances. Thus the spectacle of Christians finding amusement in gambling and Church funds deriving profit therefrom will act as an incentive and encouragement to others to gamble too much. To allow gambling as a means of raising money for charitable or Church purposes is to set a public seal of approval on gambling which will almost certainly be interpreted by some as an approval of every kind and degree of gambling.

It is impossible not to sympathize with this position. And if gambling be at the present moment a national vice so that there is a moral certainty that any condonation of it or even any action which might be interpreted as condonation of it will lead others into sin, then this position is the right one.

The Church and individual Christians must have nothing to do with gambling in any shape or form. Just as, if drunkenness were a national vice, it would become the duty of individual Christians to abstain from all public consumption of alcohol and of the Church to forbid its sale at any function or in any building under its control. Not because the Church or Christians hold that the consumption of alcohol is inherently wrong, but because in the circumstances its use would be a positive encouragement to the "weaker brethren" in what has become for them a vice.

Everything turns on whether gambling in England to-day is or is not a national vice. If it is, then Christians and the Church should have nothing to do with it—at any rate in public. Nothing must be done which will cause others to sin. If it is not, then it is unreasonable and over-rigorous to require a total abstention from a legitimate amusement just because a relatively small number of people may perversely twist that action into a justification of their own excess. The point is that where most people gamble too much, and gambling is commonly understood to mean excessive gambling, then any apparent approval of gambling will be taken to imply an approval of excessive gambling. But when most people gamble moderately, within due limits, then apparent approval of gambling can only be construed into condonation of excessive gambling by an act of wilful perversity. And for such perversity the Church and Christians cannot reasonably be blamed. In such circumstances it would be wholly legitimate for Christians to find a moderate amusement in gambling, and for the Church to use this form of amusement for the purpose of raising money.

Indeed that form of gambling which consists in such things as raffles at bazaars is probably the least dangerous of all forms. For it provides that element of surprise and expectation which is the peculiar pleasure of gambling, and is yet, of all forms of gambling, the furthest removed from avarice. The kind of thing which one usually stands to gain from a raffle or a guessing competition—a cake, a doll or a season ticket at the local theatre—is not the kind of thing which easily breeds avarice. It is not easy to believe that such amusement can be sinful, or that—except where excessive gambling is widespread and universal—it can set a bad example.

The conclusion, then, must be that although many Christians sincerely hold that all forms of gambling are inherently sinful, no convincing reasons for this view have been advanced. It seems, rather, that gambling, within due limits, is a legitimate recreative amusement. Nevertheless, it is an amusement of low cultural and recreative value, and one which is peculiarly liable to excess with the gravest consequences of moral deterioration and corruption. For this reason, though allowed, it has never been much encouraged in the Christian tradition. Further, it may at times get such a grip upon a whole people that it becomes for a while a charitable duty for all Christians totally to abstain from it, lest their innocent amusement should ever seem to justify the common excessive indulgence. In the view of many, such a position obtains in England to-day.

CHAPTER VII

SEX AND MARRIAGE

IT follows from the doctrine of God as creator that in the strictest sense of ownership man owns nothing—not even his own body. Man is in the position of trustee or tenant for life. The ownership of all created things is in God, their creator. Man has the enjoyment and the use of them, but subject always to the laws of God. They are only rightly used when they are used for the purposes for which God created them. Another way of saying the same thing is to insist that in all his use of created things man must remember their source and accord to them their proper reverence and respect as creatures of God. Christian ethics has laid particular emphasis on this in connection with the human body. The body is the earthly vehicle of expression for the human personality who is "made in the image of God" and is destined for an eternal existence in the communion of saints in heaven. While the body is alive, that is, so long as it is the vehicle of expression of the individual, it is so closely associated with him that it is only with difficulty that we distinguish between them.

I and my body are so closely interwoven and react so powerfully and intimately upon one another that we present to other people and at most levels of thoughts to ourselves a single object. Certainly it is only with the greatest difficulty that we can think of the one apart from the other. Thus it is that a corpse is naturally accorded the respect and dignity which are due to a living person. It is for this reason that the mutilation of dead bodies is abhorent and is condemned. Thus it is that the dead are buried or cremated with every mark of respect and thereafter left inviolate. Respect for dead bodies is respect for the dead whose bodies they are; it is the proper respect due to a man made in the image of God, and by adoption His son. The parallel to this instinctive respect for the dead in the case of the living body is the instinct of modesty and of chastity.

As regards other persons modesty is an instinctive recognition that their bodies cannot rightly be used as mere instruments of our pleasure : to do so is to violate the sacred rights of the person whose bodies they are. As regards ourselves, modesty is an instinctive recognition that the body and its senses are not mere organs of pleasure, but the means by which and in which we express ourselves—the means, indeed, by which and in which our personality, our very self, comes into being and growth. Modesty and delicacy are an instinctive natural protection against the degradation of the self which inevitably follows from a misuse of its vehicle of expression. The arousing of the instinct of modesty is a danger signal, a warning that that which has aroused it is, or has the appearance of being, or opens the door to, a misuse of the body. It is not an infallible guide, for there is such a thing as false modesty and over-delicacy. But it is always a warning.

The body, its parts and organs are only rightly used for the purpose for which they were created. The powers of speech, for example, exist in order to enable men more easily to live together in society. It is by speech that we enter into each other's lives, that by love and friendship we strengthen each other. It is by speech that we divide among each other the varied duties and obligations of society. It is by speech that we share and advance discovery, knowledge and wisdom. All use of speech which promotes the welfare of society is a right use of speech : all use which, like lying, tends to disrupt, to injure or to weaken the bonds of society is a wrong use of speech. Or again, the appetites of hunger and thirst and the means of satisfying them exist to maintain the body in strength and health. Food and drink taken at such times and in such quantities as shall maintain a healthy physical condition are a right use of these appetites. Drunkenness and gluttony are a wrong use of them precisely because so far from keeping the body strong and healthy they make it weak and sickly. They defeat the very end for which the appetites exist.

Thus the right use of the sexual functions of the body will depend on the purpose for which these functions have been created. It seems self-evident that the human race is divided into two sexes for the purpose of propagation. Reduced to its barest essentials the sexual organs constitute a mechanism whereby the male seed is produced on the one hand, the female egg on the other and the two are brought into conjunction. From this conjunction springs a new unit. Furthermore, the sexual organs in the male and female are so constituted as to provide a complicated but complementary mechanism whereby the seed and the egg may be brought into contact. That the propagation of the race is the primary purpose of the division into sexes and of the particular structure of the male and female sexual organs seems to be a proposition which stands beyond need of proof.

But the matter cannot be left there. If it were, any and every union of two persons of opposite sex, provided that it followed the pattern of the mechanism and so was apt for generation, would be a legitimate use of our sexual powers. The breeding of men would be as the breeding of cats and dogs. But it is manifestly not so. The human reason or conscience has at all levels of development condemned merely promiscuous unions. The reason is clear. Men do not, like animals, live only on a physical and instinctive plane. They are endowed with reason. The sexual act is not for them a simple instinctive reaction to a stimulus, it is an act of conscious choice. Even at its very lowest all human beings understand by the word love something different from what they know as "lust." The difference is the difference between the merely physical or animal and the human and rational.

Love, the emotion experienced by two human beings drawn towards each other sexually, is best understood at its highest, not at its lowest level. Though clearly rooted in the physical attractions of the persons for each other it infinitely transcends them. It adds to the physical attractions, truly or falsely, moral and spiritual qualities and because of them finds the physical attractions yet more attractive. Though desirous of the physical union, it attaches far more importance to the moral and spiritual union which the physical union would express or symbolize. The goal is not only nor so much the mutual possession of their bodies, as the interpenetration of mind and spirit, a sharing of hopes and fears and sorrows and joys. The persons in love seek through union at every level and in every part of life an escape from the loneliness of individuality into the joys of companionship. They seek with a greater or less degree of consciousness a fusion of their two personalities, that they may become together one.

Yet the physical sexual drive with which the thing started remains strong and even dominant, at any rate in the earlier stages. It is only later that it sinks into the background, when the fusion of the personalities, the moral and spiritual union, has become something of a reality. At the outset the two people in love believe, and rightly believe, that the sexual side of their relationship is all-important. Their physical union is the symbol, the expression and the creative instrument of their ever developing moral union. All this is but to say that for human beings sex is not a merely physical thing. Its use is an intensely personal moral act. It is misused except where it is expressive of a desire for the closest and most enduring, most all-embracing union possible.

There are, then, two grounds on which Christian ethics condemns promiscuity. The first has to do with the primary object of sex, the procreation of children. It is obvious that the young of the human species grow to maturity very slowly. It is only after some years that a child is capable of physical survival without the aid and support of adults. If account be taken of the child's moral and spiritual growth and education, the period of dependence is a very long one. And this process of growth into adult maturity requires the full care and attention of both its parents. It is extremely difficult for either parent alone both to provide food and shelter and also to guide the moral and intellectual development of the child. And that development itself, if it is not to be warped and biased, requires the distinctive influence and contribution of both father and mother.

The evil of promiscuity lies in this, that in itself it makes no sort of provision whatever for the nurture and upbringing, by the joint care of both of its parents acting together, of any child which may result from it. It is of the essence of such casual matings that the couple meet and separate; their union lasts no longer than the physical sexual act, and is not intended to. The same charge lies against the sexual union outside marriage of couples who are genuinely in love with one another and who intend their liaison to be of a long duration. Their circumstances are such that they cannot fulfil together as man and wife their joint responsibilities as father and mother. If it is not so, their conduct is irrational and absurd. They should marry. It is the fact that for one reason or another they cannot marry which gives to their sexual intercourse its evil quality as an offence against the offspring which may result from it.

The second ground—and in these days, when contraceptives are easily obtained and commonly used, perhaps the more relevant ground—for the condemnation of promiscuity concerns the nature of such unions. The sexual act should express and promote a desire for the closest possible union between two persons. It is an intensely personal act. It involves the giving of oneself to another particularly and ardently desired person: it involves the possession of that other person. It symbolizes and expresses the desire for the mingling of two lives to the enrichment of them both, by a mutual giving and receiving. It is of the essence of promiscuous casual matings that they express no such desire at all. What should be the sacrament of a high and noble emotion is prostituted to the use of a fleeting interest or of a degraded pursuit of physical sensation. That which should be intensely personal is made as impersonal as possible. The two who come together in such matings care little if at all about the identity of the other. It is enough that each finds in the other a means of satisfying a physical instinct.

Even where this is not true, and the union is the result and the expression of a genuine mutual love, yet because it takes place in circumstances which do not allow of the permanence of the union and its continuing growth and development, it carries within itself its own imperfection. If there are no such circumstances, the very fact that the couple do not marry is evidence that one or both do not intend by the act of sexual union that complete union and surrender which it should express. If there are such circumstances, the sexual act is only a pretence and a make-believe. It is, of course, less sinful, less a corruption and perversion than casual promiscuity : but it is still a corruption. For the act cannot lead where it should. The circumstances which prevent marriage at the same time ensure that the union shall of necessity be but partial. Something has to be held back.

It is for these reasons that the Christian tradition condemns what is known as "anticipating the marriage ceremony." Though here it is important to be clear as to what precisely is condemned. In the old days, if a couple became engaged and then had sexual relations they were deemed to have become married. And very reasonably, for by their act they had fulfilled their previously declared intention of marrying one another. They had done nothing intrinsically wrong. They had only completed their desire to give themselves to each other in marriage, by performing that physical act which is the sacrament—the efficacious sign—of the union of two lives. The Church held them to be thereby bound to each other for life in marriage. It is true that she also required them to signify publicly in Church their marriage, by going through the marriage ceremony afterwards. But that was for the sake of the children, that their legitimacy might never be called in question, and of society, that everyone might know that they were man and wife.

As time passed it was found necessary, for various reasons, to recognize only marriages which had been publicly contracted. Consequently these "anticipations of the marriage ceremony" by engaged couples were no longer deemed to establish a marriage, so that it remained open to either of the persons to break off the union at any moment if they wanted to. This altered the whole character of the act. It was no longer the final and irrevocable giving of themselves to each other, the seal and pledge of their union. It assumed a tentative, experimental quality, something from which either could if they wished draw back. It is this which the Christian tradition condemns in pre-marriage sexual relations. The sexual union should commit those whom it unites to the irrevocable responsibilities of parenthood and the permanent joining of their lives; for those are the two inherent purposes which it carries within itself.

Marriage, as the Christian tradition understands it, is the exercise of the sexual function within the limitation of these two purposes; and the tradition forbids engaged couples to join themselves sexually together—or to engage in those ancillary sexual actions which serve as a stimulus and preparation for the marital act and have no other legitimate purpose—unless and until by the marriage ceremony they have explicitly bound themselves to those two purposes; that is, to a life-long partnership and to the responsibilities of parenthood if children be born. Once they are so bound and committed the way is open for their sexual union to be both the sign and seal of their desire and the instrument of its fruition. It expresses what they want, and brings what they want into being.

It should by now be abundantly clear that the vigilance with which the Christian tradition guards the institution of marriage and the severity with which it condemns all extra-marital sexual relations proceed from the very exalted view which it holds of the nature and purpose of sex. It is in no way based upon a merely negative dislike of sex as something physical, animal, degraded. There have been some Christian teachers, it is true, who have so exalted virginity at the expense of marriage that their doctrine has the appearance of a total condemnation of everything which has to do with sex as being intrinsically evil. But the authentic Christian note is struck by St. Paul, who does not shrink from comparing the mating of men and women with the union between Christ and His Church. We shall return to this comparison later. It is enough to say here that no more exalted view of sex is conceivable, and that all the restrictions which Christian ethics imposes on its use proceed from a deep reverence for what may not improperly be called the holiness of sex as rightly used.

It is often thought that Christian ethics particularly condemns the keen physical pleasure which accompanies sex. Not even this is true. That pleasure is an irreplaceable vehicle for conveying and expressing the deep and powerful emotions which centre round sex. In itself it is good. Yet it is, perhaps, true that the Christian tradition mistrusts it because of its intensity. It so easily wins for itself a position of disproportionate influence, driving men to a misuse of their sexual powers in pursuit of it. Only too often are men enslaved by it, becoming the restless victims of an insatiable appetite which grows by what it feeds on.

Christian ethics condemns the pleasure of sex—venereal pleasure as it is called—when it is made the sole end of sexual activity to the exclusion of everything else. The essence of sexual immorality or vice lies here, in the employment of an activity which of its nature looks outward towards another person, solely for the end of a private personal satisfaction. That is to use another person as a mere means to one's own bodily enjoyment, and to make into an end in itself a pleasure which properly exists only to accompany and serve the deep purposes of sex—parenthood and unity. Such a reversal of values is wrong as well inside marriage as outside. It is only too often forgotten that in Christian ethics marriage is not a licence to uncontrolled sexual activity. There is such a thing as married chastity; it is the controlled use of sex by husband and wife for the expression of their love for one another, the deepening of their life-partnership and the creation of a family. Such married chastity leads to a permanent enrichment of both their personalities as they complete one another, to a strengthening and deepening of their mutual affection and, if it be so, to the lasting joys of parenthood. It is the meaning and the essence of marriage.

A marriage is brought into being when the parties to it contract to marry each other. It is their mutual exchange of vows which creates the marriage; the moment that each has said to the other "I take thee to be my wedded husband (or wife)" they are married. Yet the law of both Church and State require that this mutual exchange of vows or contract to marry should be made publicly and after the observance of certain formalities. The reason for these formalities and this publicity is first that every reasonable precaution may be taken to ensure that the two persons are actually able to marry each other. Therefore the fact that they are about to marry is published far and wide among their friends and acquaintances so that if anybody knows any reason why they ought not to marry, the matter can be investigated. For it is a bad thing for them and for their children if people attempt to marry, and then later find out that they were not able to marry and so are not in fact married at all. The second reason is that the marriage having been publicly contracted before witnesses the fact of the marriage is established for all time. It can be easily and decisively proved if either of the two persons or anybody else attempts later to deny it.

The marriage, then, is effected by the mutual exchange of vows before witnesses. The persons who make the marriage are the persons who are marrying. It is not the priest in church nor the registrar in his office; they are only witnesses. And a marriage in a registry office is just as much a marriage, and carries with it the same privileges, duties and responsibilities as a marriage in Church. Indeed a marriage between two Christian people in a registry office is just as much a Christian marriage and a sacrament as a marriage in Church. Of course Christian people ought to marry in Church, because they ought to desire to receive God's blessing openly and explicitly on such a momentous occasion in their lives, and the Church ordains that they shall so marry. Nevertheless, if they disobey and are married in a registry office, it is still a Christian marriage.

There are, however, certain conditions to be fulfilled if the exchange of vows is to create a marriage, and if any of them are not fulfilled then there is no marriage. Of the first of these conditions we have already spoken. There must be certain formalities observed before marriage, and a certain publicity at the marriage. The second condition is that both the parties must be able to contract marriage. It is only common sense that children below the age of adolescence cannot marry. They do not understand about sex, and they are not physically capable of the sexual act. At what age children acquire such knowledge and power of course varies with different races and customs, and indeed with different children. And so in each state the Law lays down the age below which everybody is deemed to be a child and incapable of marriage.

In England it is sixteen. Anybody in England under sixteen who marries is only "going through a marriage ceremony"; their vows and promises cannot set up an actual marriage. They have to wait till they are sixteen and then marry again or "renew their consent" as the law books call it. In the same way grown-up people who are physically incapable of the sexual act obviously cannot marry in the ordinary sense. And if, after they have married, their partner applies to a judge and this physical incapacity is proved to have existed at the time of the marriage, the marriage is set aside; it is declared null and void, never to have been a marriage.

The two persons may be unable to marry each other for a quite different reason. They may be too closely related to one another by blood or marriage. If a man exchange marriage vows with his sister, for example, or his step-mother, whether he knows what he is doing or not, it will not set up a marriage. There is a natural bar to such a union; it evokes an instinctive repugnance and is condemned by the universal conscience of mankind. It is everywhere agreed that persons related in certain ways cannot marry each other, and the laws of particular countries lay down precisely what those relationships are. A third reason why people may not be able to marry is because they are married already to someone else. But as this involves the question of divorce, we will leave it for later consideration.

The third condition which has to be satisfied is that the two persons who are marrying are doing so freely, of their own free will and consent. The vows set up no marriage if one of the persons making them is doing so under compulsion. If, for example, her parents have brought excessive influence to bear on their daughter to make her marry the man of their choice, or if the bridegroom has carried off his bride and forces her to marry him with threats, the marriage will be null and void. Because the consent on both sides must be free and full, ignorance and fraud can in some cases make the marriage void. If, for example, the man thinks he is marrying one girl, Miss X, and finds that in fact he has married Miss Y instead. Or if the girl he is marrying is pregnant by some other man and he has been told nothing about it. But it must be clearly understood that it is not any kind of fraud and deceit which vitiates a marriage. The law lays down precisely what kinds do. In general people marry each other for better or for worse, and they marry one another as they are, not as they suppose or hope them to be. Thus if the lady falsely makes herself out to be an heiress and tricks her man that way into marrying her, the marriage is good and it stands. For the man was marrying *her*, not her money.

The last condition to be satisfied is that the two persons agree to marry, and are not agreeing to something else. It can nearly always be taken for granted that this condition has been fulfilled, because in the actual vows which they exchange when they marry people explicitly say that they are taking each other for man and wife, that is, that they are marrying each other. And we all have to assume that people understand what they are saying and mean what they are saying, especially when they are saying it in a particularly solemn way and in front of witnesses. Still, it can sometimes happen that people resolve beforehand that though they are going to say the marriage promises, they are not going to mean them, but are going to intend by them something quite different.

For example, they might agree together that the moment either of them got tired of being married, or met someone else they would rather be married to, they should be absolutely free to part and get a divorce. With such an agreement in their minds and clearly understood between them, they are not, of course, marrying at all. They are doing just what a man does when he takes a mistress, or a woman a lover. The whole point about such associations, and the way in which they differ from marriage, is exactly that, that they leave both persons quite free to end the association at any time they like. Or again, one or other of the parties might stipulate, and it might be agreed, that in spite of being married there should be no sexual relations between them, and that the marriage was not to give the wife any right to expect her husband to make love to her or vice versa. But marriage *is* the conferring on the husband by the wife and on the wife by the husband of the right to sexual intercourse. And if they have ruled out the conferring of these rights, then whatever else they have done it is at least certain that they have not agreed and consented to marry.

This is a point, however, about which it is very important to be careful and clear. It is one thing to refuse to confer on each other the mutual right which constitutes marriage. That certainly makes the marriage contract void. It is quite another thing to refrain, after marriage, from ever claiming the right; it is quite another thing, even, to agree together that whilst conferring the right neither in fact will actually claim it. In either case it would be a valid marriage, even though an unconsummated one. It is quite another thing, also, to confer the right, and then subsequently refuse to grant it. That too would leave the validity of the marriage unimpaired. I have stressed this point rather heavily, because of its relevance to the confusion and perplexity which has been introduced into England by the new provision in English law that a marriage may be declared null because of a "wilful refusal to consummate" it. We will return to that in a moment.

Another agreement which would vitiate a marriage is a resolve before marriage never to have children. Before the days of easy and reliable contraceptives, such a resolve meant an intention never to have sexual intercourse; nowadays it would more probably take the form of a resolve only to have sexual intercourse with contraceptives. Such a resolve would vitiate the marriage, because the mutual right to sexual intercourse which marriage is, is a right to sexual intercourse in the natural act; the act which is of itself and inherently apt for procreation. It is not a right to any kind of sexual act, to mutual masturbation, for example, or to any form of "unnatural vice" but to the natural act, the sexual activity intended by nature; and that activity tends naturally towards the procreation of children. A resolve, therefore, never to have children but always to use contraceptives is a resolve not to confer the right of sexual intercourse, and so is a resolve, in effect, not to marry.

A great deal of confusion has been introduced by the new English ground for nullity, "wilful refusal to consummate." The confusion arises first in this way. A ground for nullity should mean something which was present before and at the moment of marriage which prevented it from ever becoming a marriage at all; the non-fulfilment of one or other of those conditions which we have been considering. But a wilful refusal to consummate is something which can only arise *after* the marriage. It might, conceivably, be a ground for divorce, but not a ground for saying that there never was a marriage. It could only be a ground for that if it were held to be final, sufficient and decisive evidence of an explicit fully-informed intention prior to marriage never to consummate the marriage. As we have seen, such an intention might vitiate the marriage. But it is quite clear that wilful refusal to consummate does not provide conclusive evidence of such an intention at all. There are all sorts of ways in which it might happen that a man married with every intention of consummating his marriage, but was for a time prevented by circumstances from doing so and then changed his mind and decided never to consummate it at all.

The second way in which confusion has arisen is over the difficulty of saying whether a refusal to have sexual intercourse without contraceptives is a refusal to consummate marriage or not. In one case (Cowan *v.* Cowan, 61, *The Times*, L.R. 525) the divorce judge said that intercourse with contraceptives did consummate the marriage. There was an appeal and the appeal court said that it did not, and that the refusal of the husband to dispense with contraceptives amounted to a wilful refusal to consummate (173 L.T.Rep. 176). This was, I think, technically a right decision, but it was obviously also dangerous and disturbing. For it meant that any married couple who had always used contraceptives had only to shew that one or other of them had consistently or frequently urged their discontinuance, and they would get their marriage put aside. And in most cases the only possible evidence would be that of the parties themselves. A wide field was open for collusion. The matter has not been allowed to rest there. In a case which went on appeal to the House of Lords, the House of Lords decided that sexual intercourse with contraceptives did consummate a marriage in the sense which Parliament intended by consummation in the 1927 Marriage Act. This, though plainly contrary, I think, to the true and proper meaning of consummation, has the effect of forestalling the danger inherent in the former judgement; and for the purpose of administering English marriage law it is in that respect and to that extent a good decision. But in making the judgement the Lord Chancellor argued that the use or not of contraceptives was irrelevant because procreation is not the primary end of marriage (Baxter *v.* Baxter, 2.All. E.R. 886 (1947)). This is quite certainly contrary to all traditional Christian teaching. That teaching holds, as we have seen, that the natural end or tendency of sexual intercourse is procreation, and that marriage is the right to have that sexual intercourse. In that sense the procreation of children is the primary end of marriage beyond all doubt. It is not, of course, the sole end of marriage, nor indeed the sole end of sexual intercourse. But it is the primary end in the sense that it is that which gives to it its essential character, that which primarily explains it. And sexual intercourse of such a character as not to be of itself apt for procreation, but in some artificial way deprived of its natural efficacy is not the sexual intercourse to which marriage confers the right and is not a consummation of marriage.

All the confusion would have been avoided if wilful refusal to consummate had been made a ground for divorce instead of nullity. In the pre-Reformation Church law, as in Roman Catholic canon law now, it is recognized as such : at least in the simpler and more logical form of non-consummation. A valid but unconsummated marriage may by that law be dissolved for good reasons. A marriage where there had been intercourse with contraceptives might not be regarded as one that ought to be so dissolved, but where consummation had been prevented by some accident—a tragic separation, or some physical mishap—relief of a divorce would be granted and the two people set free to marry elsewhere.

This brings us to the subject of divorce. The law of England, of course, recognizes only monogamous marriage. You cannot, by English law, be married to two persons at the same time. If you try to be, not only is the second marriage null and void, but you have committed a felony. Yet English law allows for the dissolution of a marriage on certain grounds, so that both the parties are thereby free to make other marriages, without committing bigamy. The law of the Western Church, however, though permitting, as we have seen, the occasional dissolution of an unconsummated marriage, maintains that no power on earth can dissolve a valid and consummated marriage. Those who marry and consummate their marriage, marry until death do them part; a relationship is established between them which nothing but death can destroy.

This doctrine rests in part on a deduction from what are called "the principles of natural law." On the one hand, the nurture and upbringing of children is a slow process; further, second and third children are born long before the first is become independent, and the responsibilities of parenthood in this way cover the whole period of sexual potency, in the case of the mother if not of the father. This natural fact requires, for the good of the children, that the parents remain together discharging their duties for their lifetimes. On the other hand, if we consider the second purpose of sex—what may be called, perhaps, the sacrament of love—we reach a similar conclusion. The sexual act is the expression of a desire for the closest possible union and inter-dependence.

The achievement of this union on the moral and spiritual plane is a slow and difficult business. It is subject to constant set-backs and disappointments. What at the outset seems so easy because so ardently desired, is seen after a little to be not easy at all. There are inevitable disagreements between husband and wife, of major and minor importance, which have to be harmonized. There are many adjustments of personal habits, interests and preferences, which have to be made in order that husband and wife may accommodate themselves to each other and live in amicable union. There are many revelations of hidden character and temperament to be accepted, and understood, and a new and revised picture of each other's personality to be assimilated. There is the contempt and staleness which familiarity is apt to bring; this has to be lived through and transmuted into the stable affection and quiet trust of a long and well-tried partnership.

These and the many other trials of married life together with all its shared joys and sorrows are the stuff out of which is built up that intimate union, unfailing sympathy and deep understanding which are the glory and hallmark of a happy marriage. It is above all else important that a husband and wife as they travel this road, travel it in the certainty that there is no other road. The certainty that there is no alternative to living together—except the dreary loneliness of separation—provides them with an invaluable external support against temptations to despair and the illusory enticements of other unions. In other words, if the sex act is to fulfil its second purpose as the expression and vehicle of union on the moral and spiritual plane as well as on the physical, the relationship must be rigorously confined to one man with one woman. That is, marriage is strictly monogamous because sex is more than physical: sex effects a physical union as an expression of a moral union which has still to be brought into being.

For Christians the final answer to this question is to be sought and found in Scripture. The inadmissibility of remarriage after divorce is expressly laid down by our Lord Himself. He is reported as having said "Whosoever shall put away his wife and marry another committeth adultery, and whosover marries her that is put away committeth adultery." It is true that one passage in St. Matthew's Gospel (chap. xix,

v. 9) suggests at first sight a limitation and mitigation of this sweeping condemnation. But it is now generally agreed among New Testament scholars that (1) this apparent exception cannot be regarded as forming part of our Lord's authentic teaching, (2) that in the context in which it appears, it has no general application but is an answer to one specific question, namely, "to which of two rival Rabbinic rulings would our Lord attach himself?" and (3) that the meaning of "except for fornication " is ambiguous, but almost certainly does not mean infidelity after marriage. The conclusion, therefore, stands that our Lord unreservedly condemned re-marriage after divorce, and condemned it on the ground that it is a form of adultery.

This conclusion is supported by the practice of the undivided Church which for four hundred years prohibited its members from marrying after divorce, and that in the face of a violently hostile contemporary secular opinion. It is further and finally supported by St. Paul who states that the commandment of the Lord is "Let not the wife depart from her husband ; but and if she depart, let her remain unmarried or be reconciled to her husband ; and let not the husband put away his wife." (I Cor. vii, 10-11.) From this position the eastern Church has considerably departed, under the influence of Roman civil law, and it permits divorce with the right of re-marriage for a number of causes. The western Church, on the other hand, of which the Church of England is a part, has at any rate in theory remained consistently loyal to our Lord's prohibition. By the law of the western Church husband and wife are bound indissolubly together throughout their joint lives. They may not separate from one another permanently except for the gravest reasons and by the permission of authority.

The Church does not recognize, as English law recognizes, the right of married people to agree together to separate. For married people are under mutual obligations to one another from which they have no authority to discharge themselves. Nevertheless in cases of great hardship and danger they may be freed from the duty of fulfilling some of the obligations of marriage. That is to say, it is sometimes right to ask for a separation order : indeed it is sometimes right to apply for a decree of divorce. What the Church unreservedly and in all circumstances forbids is not a separation or a divorce but the contracting of a new marriage, which by the fresh duties and obligations thereby created finally and irrevocably bars the doors against any reconciliation and renewal of partnership between the two persons originally and truly married to each other.

A second marriage makes it impossible to continue loyal to the first marriage. But the first marriage is like the union between Christ and His Church. This pregnant comparison expresses more vividly and more fully than anything else the Christian doctrine of marriage. In the first place the purpose of the Incarnation, that is of the union of Christ with His Church, is the re-creation of the human race. The salvation of souls, the gathering of them into the ark of the Covenant is the first end of Christ's indwelling within His Church. In the second place, the union of Christ and the Church is the closest possible inter-penetration. He is her life : she is His Body. It is impossible to think of the Church apart from Christ, or of Christ without His Church.

As there is no limit to the patience and sacrifice with which Christ gives Himself to the Church, nor to the loyalty and suffering with which the Church should remain constant and faithful to her Lord, so there is no limit to the joy of the Lord in His Church nor to the peace and happiness of the Church in her Lord. There is no part of the Church's life which is not governed and permeated by the presence of the Lord : and for His part, He gives Himself to the Church whose members are by adoption no less than the sons of God. Here is the true pattern to which marriage should conform. It seeks to create a family ; it effects the closest possible union between husband and wife, governing every part of their joint lives. Rooted in a mutual love which is essentially sacrificial, it demands a loyalty which neither prosperity can corrupt nor adversity destroy, a fidelity which no humiliation, no insult, no ingratitude can overcome. The grace which the sacrament of marriage gives to Christians is the power of God to realize—that is, to make come true—

in each particular marriage the true purpose and nature of all marriage; the power to make of human love and of a human union a not unworthy picture of the divine love for men and of Christ's dwelling within His Church.

CHAPTER VIII

THE SANCTITY OF HUMAN LIFE

At all levels of human culture and development conscience has sought to check the propensity which men have to kill each other in anger or in revenge. The degree of success attained is one of the clearest standards for measuring the cultural level of any given society. A high value attached to human life, the prohibition or restraint of any private and unauthorized taking of human life and a strict legal control of authorized executions are the marks of an advanced civilization. The Christian tradition inherited from its Jewish antecedents the divine commandment "Thou shalt not kill," to which it has added its own insights. The doctrine of the Incarnation has made clearer the infinite value of every individual human being. The doctrine of the Cross has revealed the mercy with which divine justice is ever accompanied and has enjoined on all men the duty to forgive as they are themselves forgiven. The right to life is the final ultimate right which all men enjoy. And no man may justly deprive his neighbour of this. Consequently Christian societies have in general and at least in theory provided for all their members, even for the least privileged, a high degree of personal safety. Christian ethics commands men to preserve their own lives, and the lives of those for whom they are responsible. It forbids them to kill themselves or to attack one another unjustly.

The prohibition of suicide is derived from the doctrine of God as Creator. Man is not the author of his own life: he has received it from God. It is given him for use, and its destruction is a direct violation and negation of the purpose for which God has given it. Man is created by God to serve Him in the body in this life. The period of that service is not for man to determine. Suicide therefore is a grave offence against God who is the author and preserver of our life. It is also an offence against proper self-love; in all men there is implanted a natural instinct of self-preservation, and to use our powers to destroy ourselves is to use them in direct violation of their natural purpose. Lastly, suicide is an offence against society. Each man has a duty towards the society of which he is a member, namely to be a useful member of it; and by suicide he deprives society prematurely of those services and benefits which it has a right to expect from him.

Suicide may be direct or indirect. That is, one may kill oneself by a direct voluntary and positive act. Or one may perform an act which does not itself directly cause death, but which creates a very grave danger or even a certainty of death. In the Christian tradition direct suicide is never permissible. Indirect suicide is sometimes allowable when there are correspondingly weighty reasons. For example, nobody doubts the legitimacy, indeed the heroism, of those who sacrifice themselves for the good of others—as Captain Oates exposed himself to the certain risk of death by walking out into the Antarctic cold, or as the winners of the George Cross put themselves in the way of certain death to save others. The point is that in such cases the action performed is only the indirect cause of death; the ensuing death is indeed foreseen, but it is not the direct object of the will, not something chosen for its own sake. The death is permitted as an inevitable secondary consequence of an act performed for a quite different reason. But if such an act is to be right, the reason for performing it must be a very serious one. No one is justified in risking his life for a trifle. And the greater the risk, the greater must be the justifying reason. But, to make the point once more, no reason is great enough to justify a man in deliberately and directly taking his life. That is never legitimate. What is sometimes legitimate is to expose oneself to a grave risk or even certainty of death as an indirect consequence of something that we do.

To the general prohibition of the taking of human life, the Christian tradition has always made three exceptions.

The first of these is the right of each individual to self-defence. There is a natural right inherent in every man to defend his life against an unjust aggressor. The command to love our neighbours and the command "resist not evil" do not abrogate this right. They do, however, control it; for they impose stringent conditions on its exercise.

It is not lawful to kill another man, even in self-defence, unless it is absolutely necessary and the attack is unjust. Thus it is not legitimate to kill a policeman in self-defence, because a policeman is acting justly when he attempts an arrest. The condition of absolute necessity means that if we can avoid being killed by running away or by calling for help we must do so, and we should be guilty morally of murder if instead we kill our assailant. Secondly, it means that we must be subjected to actual murderous assault and not merely to the threat of one, before we are justified in killing the aggressor. But an actual assault may be taken to include the immediate preparation for one, such as the drawing of a revolver or a knife coupled with a menacing attitude. Thirdly, it means that the killing of our assailant is the only way, or the only really safe way, of preserving our own life. Hence if we can with reasonable certainty save ourselves by wounding the aggressor we are morally bound to take that course; and we are never justified in killing him after we have disabled him. That would be an act, not of self-defence, but of revenge. The law of love totally forbids revenge and personal vindictiveness. If it be necessary in self-defence to kill another man, it is forbidden to intend his death directly. What we intend is the preservation of our own life; his death is an, in the circumstances, unavoidable consequence of that. Hence the invariable rule that in defending ourselves we must never use more violence than is absolutely necessary.

It is, of course, true that in the emergency of a murderous assault no one can be expected to be very clear-headed and precise in his estimation of what degree of force is in fact necessary to repel it. A man is not to be harshly judged if in a moment of fear he shoots to kill when he should have shot to wound. Yet it is important to stress the fact that the exception to the law forbidding to kill, which the Christian tradition makes in the case of self-defence, is not an indiscriminate one. Above all it is important to remember that the death of the aggressor is never to be directly willed in itself, but only permitted as an inevitable consequence of preserving our own life. This right to kill in self-defence is only a right, it is not a duty. No one is bound to preserve his life in this way, but he may if he wishes permit himself to be killed.

This right to kill has been extended, with the same limitations, to the defence of others who are being attacked, and to the preservation of property. We may, though we are not always bound to, come to the rescue of another and save him even at the cost of killing his assailant. But as with self-defence, the killing is only justified when it is absolutely necessary. The extension of this permission to the defence of property seems more questionable. At no time has killing been held to be justified unless the property defended was of very considerable value to its owner. And it was always required that no other means existed of preventing the theft. In a modern community with a highly organized police force the question is not likely to arise. It will generally be possible to procure the thief's arrest or at least the recovery of the property by calling in the police, and the killing of the thief in the act of his theft can rarely be justified in the circumstances of modern life in a civilized community. Indeed the presumption is wholly against the necessity of such action, and it is for this reason that the possession of firearms by private householders is strongly deprecated. The position is therefore that theoretically and in certain unlikely circumstances the Christian tradition holds a man to be justified in killing in defence of his property: in practice, such a resort to force is condemned. But what of the defence of one's honour?

It is generally agreed that a woman may kill the man who is attempting to rape her, if she cannot otherwise prevent his purpose. This is partly because of the exceedingly grave nature of the injustice with which she is threatened and partly because a woman subjected to such an assault is in actual danger of death; for rape is not uncommonly followed by murder. Since both honour and life are thus at stake, it is legitimate to resist even at the cost of killing the assailant. It is not legitimate to carry resistance so far when it is a case only of "indecent assault" which causes annoyance and distress but does not involve either danger to life or risk of conception.

The practice of fighting duels in defence of honour is not allowed by the Christian tradition. The practice is irrational and absurd, for a man's honour cannot in any way be preserved by the fact that he kills or wounds his opponent. There is here no sufficient reason of self-defence to justify the taking of human life.

The second great exception to the prohibition of killing is war. The general consensus of Christian opinion has consistently maintained that it is sometimes lawful to engage in war, and that in consequence for those so engaged it is lawful to kill the enemy. In the course of centuries moral theology elaborated a series of conditions and restrictions in the matter of entering upon and conducting wars. These conditions and restrictions are all derived from two main principles. First, that the only legitimate object of a war is the establishment of a just peace; and second, that only so much force be employed as is necessary for that purpose. From these principles it follows that it is never lawful to engage in war, if there is any other way of obtaining justice. Secondly, it follows that although it is lawful to fight a war to obtain a redress of injustice otherwise unobtainable, or to preserve the existence of a nation, the war ceases to be lawful the moment the enemy offers to redress the injustice, or ceases from his attacks. Thirdly, it follows that in the conduct of the war only those acts of killing and destruction are lawful which directly conduce to the winning of the war in the limited sense given above, and are essential to its prosecution. A state of war does not entitle the belligerents to practise any and every act of destruction. Fourthly, a war is only lawful if it is entered upon and conducted throughout with one purpose—the avoidance or redress of injustice and the consequent enactment of a just peace. The destruction of an enemy, or the aggrandisement of either side are not lawful objects of war. The object of a just war is to enable both parties to live together amicably after its cessation in a condition of mutual justice.

The morality of war and the laws of war are too great and too complicated a subject to be adequately dealt with here. They would need a book to themselves. They are a noble and heroic attempt to restrain the passions of men and to limit the inevitable evil consequences of war. It is often said that the whole conception of a just war and of laws of war is now out of date or academic, for experience has shown that modern war at least is not amenable to any restriction and is not to be limited either in its outbreak or in its conduct by any considerations of morality. It is undeniably true that the two great wars of this century have violated the Christian tradition in almost every respect. The consequences of that violation have been an immeasurable increase of the evil destructiveness of war. Yet one would have thought that the right conclusion to draw from that was not that the Christian teaching of the place of justice in war was untrue or even irrelevant, but that the dreadful consequences of ignoring that teaching strongly suggest its truth and relevance. It is a sinful doctrine of despair that man when he becomes engaged in war is no longer able to govern his actions in accordance with the laws of morality, that his passions and necessities must totally pervert his judgement and paralyse his will.

However this may be, the horrors of unrestricted modern warfare have produced in many parts of Christendom a strong conviction that war is in itself and in all circumstances wrong : that to take any part in war is contrary to the law of God and totally incompatible with being a Christian. The very concept of a just war is held to be a contradiction in terms. At first sight, in view of the Sermon on the Mount and other passages in Scripture this seems self-evident, and the wonder is that war ever found a place in Christian Moral Theology at all. But the Fathers were not ignorant of their Bible, and they deduced the justice of war in certain circumstances from the command to love our neighbours. From this commandment they inferred that it is the duty of those in authority to protect those whom they govern and for whom they are responsible from external enemies, so that they may live their lives in peace; and it is the duty of the governed to give them so much assistance in this task as is necessary.

Love of neighbour demands that peace be maintained, that society be stable and orderly, that all enjoy quietly the fruits of their labour living securely in their families. Whatever force is necessary to maintain such a peaceable condition is force justly and rightly used. The Fathers held that it is a strange way to show our love of our neighbour to permit him to suffer the grossest injustice while it is in our power, though at risk to ourselves, to prevent it. They had no doubt that the legions acted justly and in accordance with neighbourly love in withstanding barbarian incursions. They went further, and held that it was a strange way to show our love for our neighbour to permit him to practise the worst outrages of injustice and by such permission to encourage him. They held that it was the work and duty of love to restrain him, even by force if need be. They deemed it a work of love to show all would-be aggressors that the powers that be are ordained by God and they bear not the sword in vain.

No doubt things were simpler in those days than they are now. Yet since the end of the last war there has been more than one outbreak of fighting in which it seems that those who have been engaged in maintaining order, in protecting civilians from murder and robbery, and preventing a society from disintegrating into chaos or from losing its freedom to a group of despots, have been acting not only with courage but with justice and charity. Or are we to say that in Palestine, in Greece and in Malaya it was the clear duty of a Christian to stand aside, to let things take their course and to give no active assistance to the authorities in their efforts to maintain a free, stable and orderly society? And were those authorities wrong in all the measures which they took?

It is perhaps doubtful whether in fact extreme pacificism is widely held. When the incidence of war is restricted, and its intention of maintaining order and preventing injustice is clear—as is the cases we have just mentioned—it is probable that most people agree with the general Christian tradition of the lawfulness of war. The strength of the pacifist case is felt in the matter of a world war, or a war between two or more great powers. The case may be simply summed up in the proposition that a war between two great powers or even between one great power and the rest of the world must necessarily cause greater evils than those which it is designed to prevent or forestall. "In the changed conditions of modern war more thought should be given to the question whether any good which can issue from victory can possibly outweigh the physical, moral and spiritual evils of modern war."*

In other words, the argument is this. Granted that a refusal to engage in war will entail the setting up of an alien tyranny or the establishment of a minority government subservient to the commands and wishes of a foreign power: and granted that such a tyranny or government will involve the persecution of religion, the loss of freedom of speech and association, forced labour, fear, insecurity and all the horrors of a police state, yet even so that is a less evil than the evil of modern war. For modern war involves an appalling loss of human life and a widespread destruction of property. And that is the least of its evils. For there follows inevitably from the conditions of modern war a terrifying moral deterioration. This is caused by the general atmosphere of war with its disregard of human life, and its insecurity. Moreover, the splitting up of families with its sharp discontinuity and projection into strange and unfamiliar surroundings breaks down the normal standards of behaviour. Again, the qualities which make for success in modern war are almost diametrically opposed to those which are required for the well-being of a

---

*Minority note by the Ven. P. Hartill, Archdeacon of Stoke-on-Trent, in *The Church and the Atom*, a report of a Church Assembly Commission. This report contains a brilliant account and is itself a striking example of the traditional treatment of the subject of war in Christian Moral Theology.

society in time of peace. When the war is over, it leaves behind a grim harvest of lawlessness, crime and licence.

It is impossible to deny that there is great plausibility in this argument. And if its premisses are allowed, traditional moral theology would accept it. For it has always been agreed that war is only justified as an extreme measure, and when it is clear that the evils which it seeks to avoid are greater than those which it brings in its own train. It is an extremely difficult decision which Christians to-day are called upon to make. It is not the decision whether war is in any circumstance lawful, whether it is ever permissible in the interests of peace and justice to kill the unjust aggressor by opposing force with force. On that matter the Christian conscience is in general clear. The decision is, between two appalling evils to decide which is the less. On the one hand there is the certainty that totalitarian governments would, if their assault were unopposed, impose a regime which cynically disregards justice, is hostile to religion, and fatally destructive of most of those rights and liberties in the exercise and enjoyment of which men are enabled to live the good life. On the other hand there is the certainty that war will itself cause such appalling spiritual, moral and physical harm, that here too the conditions which make possible the living of the good life will be gravely imperilled if not destroyed.

It is probable that Christians will estimate these two evils differently, and in all honesty will come to opposite conclusions. All that can usefully be said here is that if it appears to a man certain that the evils resulting from war are greater than those involved in a surrender, he is justified in refusing to take part in a war. If he is certain that the corruption that would follow on surrender is greater than the corruption that would be engendered by the war, it is his duty to engage in the war to the utmost of his ability. If any reader wants the author's opinion and thinks it of any value, it is my own view that the voluntary acceptance of an alien tyranny would be certainly the lesser evil if the people as a whole recognized what was involved and were steeled to resist its corruptive power, at an inevitably high cost in individual moral and physical courage. I am thinking of Denmark in the last war.

On the other hand, if the surrender were dictated by cowardice and consideration of ease and comfort, I think that then it would be the greater of the evils. For it would then be almost certain that the corruptive power of tyranny would have full sway, and would produce no compensating heroism or sacrifice. There would be no passive but costly resistance to unjust and degrading laws. There would be no spiritual leaven to shame and convert the conquerors. On the contrary, conqueror and conquered would sink to ever lower levels of moral squalor, until society disintegrated in corruption. In comparison with that the horrors of war and its corruptive waging and aftermath would be preferable. But the decision is one which cannot very well be taken in advance of the circumstances which will make it acutely necessary. For the decision is a balancing of those very circumstances. And it seems to me to be clearly wrong to prejudge the issue by such a measure of national disarmament as would make resistance impossible whatever the circumstances. And there the matter had better be, most unsatisfactorily, left.

The third exception to the prohibition of killing is capital punishment. The legitimacy of capital punishment is inferred in the first place from Scripture. Not only is it to be found everywhere in the Old Testament, but it is apparently endorsed in the New. Our Lord answers Pilate's threat "Knowest thou not that I have power to crucify thee and have power to release thee?" with the admission "Thou couldest have no power at all against me except it were given thee from above." (John xix, 11.) That is, the power of a judge to sentence to death comes from God. The same teaching is given by St. Paul, "The powers that be are ordained by God . . . for he beareth not the sword in vain: for he is a minister of God, a revenger to execute wrath upon him that doeth evil." (Romans xiii, 4.) In the second place capital punishment is defended by an appeal to reason. It is put in this way by St. Thomas Aquinas. "It is lawful to kill animals in so far as animals exist for the use of men, as everything which is imperfect exists for that which is perfect. Now every part is related to its whole, as the imperfect to the perfect;

therefore every part exists for the whole. And so we see that if the safety of the whole human body requires the amputation of one limb, because, for example, it is infecting all the others, then that amputation is wholesome and praiseworthy. Now every single person stands to the total community as a part to the whole. Therefore if a particular man is dangerous to the community because he corrupts it by reason of some sin, the killing of him is wholesome and praiseworthy in order that the common good may be preserved." (Summa. II-II 64, art. 2.) That is to say, if the death of a malefactor is necessary for the good of society, it is right to kill him. Whilst it would be untrue to say that this doctrine has never been questioned by Christians—for it was denied by Waldensians and Anabaptists among others—and it is certain that the list of crimes for which death is regarded as a proper punishment has been consistently shortened, nevertheless it is only in comparatively recent times that it has been widely and passionately denied.

It is denied chiefly on two grounds. Firstly, that it contradicts the true nature of all punishment, namely the reformation of the offender. And secondly, that the taking of life goes beyond the proper limits of human power and by its example inculcates a general disregard of the value of human life.

The first argument rests on a false premise. The correction of the offender is not the sole purpose of punishment. In punishment there are three elements or purposes, the vindictive, the deterrent, and the reformative. Vindictive punishment has nothing to do with revenge. It is derived from the Latin word for punishment, vindicta. And this perhaps suggests that we have here the dominant element in the whole concept of punishment. Vindictive punishment is said to be a matter of justice, of redressing the balance which an act of injustice has disturbed. It is something which is due from, a debt which has been incurred by, him who has been guilty of an offence. The sense of justice innate in all men appears to demand that wrong-doers should be punished; and if they are not punished we say that "justice has not been done." Over and above the restoration or making good of whatever damage the act of wrong-doing may have occasioned, and over and above a sincere purpose of amendment, a resolution never to do that kind of thing again, justice appears to demand that something further be inflicted upon and accepted by the wrong-doer as a sort of payment or reparation, not for the consequence of his evil action but for the evil action itself. It is this conviction which underlies the *lex talionis*, the eye for an eye and tooth for a tooth. And it is probably the fundamental element in punishment.

Yet it is not the only element, and if it be treated as such justice itself is thwarted. Such vindictive punishment should be inflicted as will of itself tend towards the reformation of the offender. That is to say, the punishment should be such as is likely to induce in him an admission of guilt, a movement of repentance and a resolution of amendment. Thus a change of environment and the submission of the offender to reforming and educative influences form very properly a large part of the punishments which are inflicted in Christian countries. This is due in justice to the offender. For although every criminal is primarily himself responsible for his crime, society is not wholly devoid of all responsibility itself. In the very act of administering punishment it owes some reparation to the offender for the evil influences and environment to which he has been subjected and which are in part the cause of his crime.

Finally, that punishment is just which at the same time acts as a deterrent. In so doing it serves the good both of the potential offender himself and of the community in which he lives. The punishment of A is not rightly thought of as a deterrent to B. That would be to use A as a mere instrument and means of the good of B. The punishment of A is due to A. He has incurred it, knowing that he ran the risk of incurring it. The fear of it was intended to deter him. That it has failed to do. But it is still due. No consideration of B enters into it at all, except in so far as failure to inflict the punishment amounts to a declaration to B that he may commit this crime with impunity or at least without incurring this particular penalty.

In so far as the argument against capital punishment

turns on its lack of deterring power, the question is one of fact and experience. That it does not deter in all cases is of course obvious. But the strange argument is sometimes advanced that what is, *ex hypothesi*, regarded as a lesser punishment, imprisonment for life, has the same deterring power as the greater punishment of death. That is, that men fear and are restrained by the less fearful as much as by the more fearful. But however this may be the important thing from the ethical point of view is the universal admission that the community has the right to protect itself against potential criminals by the threat of punishment, and the consequent right—necessary to give to the threat its effective restraining power—of inflicting the punishment when it has been incurred.

But not, it is said, the death penalty. Because although it may have deterring power, it also makes it impossible to bring about the reformation of the offender. If by reformation be meant a life of usefulness and social virtue this is of course true. But if by reformation be meant contrition and a purpose of amendment it is by no means true. There is ample evidence of the reformation of condemned criminals, and of their acceptance of the death penalty as a just estimate of the gravity of their crime and as the proper retribution for their offence.

Yet even so, it is said, the punishment is excessive and goes beyond the proper limits of human power. This is the second argument and is the heart of the matter. It is not a question of human feelings, of pity for a man under sentence of death and of disgust at the savagery and cruelty of a society which so sentences him. For here we may observe that very often those who, out of pity, are most indignant at capital punishment, attacking it as an invasion of an inviolable human right, are also, out of pity, the most passionate advocates of euthanasia. The feelings of humanity are honourable, but they confuse the issue. And the issue is narrowed down precisely to this : is it morally right to take the life of a man guilty of a grave offence, or is it essentially wrong because a man's right to life is inviolable ? The answer to this question is not easy. There are many whose opinion on questions of ethics is entitled to the profoundest respect who are quite certain that capital punishment is for this reason wrong. Life is a gift from God, and only God may end it. And until God does end it, every man has a right to his continued existence on earth, to make such good use of it as he can or will. All that society may rightfully do to restrain him from a bad use of his life is to place him somewhere where he is no longer a nuisance. And if society finds it necessary to do that, it ought at the same time to make every effort to dissuade him from continuing to want to be a nuisance. Society has no right to put an abrupt end to his life. To do so is to take God's place as judge and perchance to rob him of that opportunity of repentance and amendment which may otherwise await him in later life. On the other side there are those who are equally certain that in some circumstances a man may properly be judged to have forfeited the right to life which otherwise all men undoubtedly enjoy.

In reply to the objection that to kill a man is in itself a wrong action, and therefore to kill a criminal cannot be right St. Thomas says that when a man does what is wrong he departs from the order of reason and so falls from the dignity of human nature as a being existing in his own right, and is rather to be equated with animals who exist not for themselves but for others. And that therefore such people are no longer necessarily to be regarded as retaining their right to be treated as an end, but may be treated as a means. Therefore, although it is certainly wrong to kill a man who is not a wrong-doer, it may be a good thing to kill a wrongdoer, just as it is good to kill an animal. For a bad man is worse than an animal, and more dangerous. (II-II 64, art, 2.) In other words, in so far as a man ceases to behave as a human being, that is as a rational and moral being, he forfeits the rights of a human being. It is presumably by some such argument as this that all punishment is justified. For every punishment violates some right. A fine is an invasion of the rights of property. Imprisonment violates the right to freedom, and the right to live with one's family in a place of one's own choosing. Such violent action by society against human rights can, surely, only be justified on the grounds that the offender has forfeited the right so invaded. Is it then unreasonable to hold that he may also forfeit the right to life itself?

It has been the general opinion of Christian people that he may. But society only rightly claims that forfeit in cases of extreme gravity. That is, only where it is held to be necessary to the peace and welfare of the community: never when some lesser penalty is adequate to protect society. For the right to life is the last and ultimate right. Put this way, the question is seen to be one not of moral principle but of administrative government. Is the state of society such that the death penalty is not needed? Are potential offenders likely to be adequately deterred by the threat of a lesser punishment? The proper charge to bring is not that society has no right to execute criminals, but that the execution of criminals is needless.

There are also other conditions with which the Christian tradition has restricted the enforcement of the death penalty. First the offence must be of the gravest character, so that society suffers from it most grievous damage—and if this condition be not fulfilled the punishment is clearly excessive and therefore unjust: the final ultimate right is not properly forfeit for a trivial injury. Secondly, there must be the most stringent proof of guilt. No man may be put to death while any doubt lingers of his guilt, still less may he be put to death on suspicion. Thirdly, the right to put a wrong-doer to death belongs not to any private individual, but is the prerogative of the supreme authority. "It is lawful to kill a malefactor," says St. Thomas, "in so far as the public safety demands it, and therefore that belongs only to him to whom is committed the burden of preserving society." (II-II 64, art. 3.) Private vengeance and lynchings find no sanction in the Christian tradition. Finally, between the sentence of the judge and the execution there must be left a decent interval of time that the condemned man may be assisted to penitence and may make his reconciliation with God.

This discussion of the three exceptions to the prohibition of the taking of human life must necessarily have distorted the picture of Christian teaching. It is right therefore to end by stressing the sanctity of human life. Both justice and charity demand that we respect each other's rights, and the greatest right is that to life itself. "Thou shalt not kill" but "Thou shalt love thy neighbour as thyself."

BIBLIOGRAPHY

CLASSICAL

Aquinas, S. Thomas. *Summa Theologica. Prime et Secunde Secundae.*
Liguori, S. Alphonso. *Theologia Moralis.*
Sanderson, Bishop R. *De Obligatione Conscientiae.*
Taylor, Bishop Jeremy. *Ductor Dubitantium.*
Baxter, Richard. *Christian Directory.*

MODERN

Prummer, Dom. M. *Manuale Theologiae Moralis* (3 vols.).
Davis, H. *Moral and Pastoral Theology* (4 vols.).
Maritain, Jacques. *True Humanism.*
────── *The Rights of Man.*
Flew, R. Newton. *The Idea of Perfection.*
Kirk, Bishop K. E. *Conscience and its Problems.*
────── *The Threshold of Ethics.*
────── *The Vision of God.*
Niebuhr, R. *The Nature and Destiny of Man* (2 vols.).
Dewar, L., and Hudson, C. E. *Christian Morals.*
Mortimer, R. C. *The Elements of Moral Theology.*

INDEX

A

ACEDIA, 40
Adultery, 74
Almsgiving, 52-3
Ambrose, St., 63
Ames, William, 58
Amusement, 97
Anger, 39-40
Appetites, human, 105
Aquinas, St. Thomas, 84, 132-3, 136
Austin, St., 63
Authority, 22-40
,, of Kings, 57-8
,, Obedience to, 58-60
Avarice, 39

B

BAXTER, RICHARD, 58, 61, 85
Behaviour :
    Christian, 7, 19-20, 22
    Communist, 7
    Nazi, 7
    pattern of, 13
Bible, 15
,, and Ethics, 7-21
Body, the human, 104

C

CHANCE, 87
Charity, duty of, 99, 103
Charles I, 57
Chrysostom, St., 63
Church, The Christian :
    Authority of, 22-40
    Attitude to moral problems, 23-5
    Membership of, 49-50
    Churchmanship, 51-2
    Disobedience in, 60
Code, Nazi, 14
Commandments, Ten, 57, 73
Conduct :
    Influence of belief on, 7
    Right, 15-6
    Christian, 22
    Commercial, 84
    (See Virtues)

Confession, seal of, 27-8
Conscience, 8, 22-40
,, Obedience to dictates of, 25-6
,, Conscientious objectors, 27
,, Supremacy of, 28-30, 36
,, "The obligation of," 57
,, Liberty of, 70
Consideration, 19
Courtesy, 19-20
Customs and Excise, 67-8

D

DEDICATION, 48
Disobedience :
    in society, 57-9
    in the Church, 60-1
Divorce, 118-121
Duels, 127
Duty :
    to God, 42
    of religion, 42-55
    of prayer, 48
    social, 72-86

E

ENVY, 39
Eucharist, 50-1
Evidence, 28-9

F

FAMILY, 57
Fasting, 53-5
Forgiveness :
    need of, 44
    of enemies, 46-7
Fortitude, 38
Freedom :
    personal, 78
    of choice, 78

G

GAMBLING, 87-103
   ,,   evils of, 97-8
   ,,   excess of, 98-103
Genesis, 8
Gluttony, 39
God :
    nature of, 7-8
    Law of, 8
Gratitude, 47

H

HAPPINESS, 9
Hedonism, 8
Humility, 18-9, 48

I

IGNORANCE, responsibility for, 32
Immortality, 42
Individual, value of, 16-7
Insurance, 89
Intercession, 46

J

JESUS CHRIST, 42
Justice, 12-13, 18, 38

L

LABOUR:
    efficiency and incentives, 76-8
    conditions of, 82-4
Law :
    Canon : reform of, 61
    Just and unjust, 68-9
    Moral, 10-11
    Marriage, 116-7
    Natural, 11, 13-4
    of evidence, 28
    obedience to, 57
    penal, 66-8
Life, human ; sanctity of, 123-138
Love :
    of God, 42
    of friends, 46
Lust, 39

M

MARRIAGE, 12, 104-122
Memory, 12
Mercy, 18
Morality, commercial, 84-6
Morals, 22
Motive, 37

N

NATURE, human, 11
Negligence, 31
Neighbour, duty to, 57

O

OATES, CAPT. 124
Obedience, 7
   ,,   to conscience, 25
   ,,   to God rather than man, 26-7, 36
   ,,   duty of, 43, 57-71
   ,,   to law, 57

P

PACIFICISM, 129
Paul, St., 63
Personality, human, 104
Peter, St., 63
Petitions, 45
Prayer :
    private, 43-8
    public, 49-50
Price, just, 48
Pride, 39
Propaganda, 33-4
Property, private :
    right to, 75-8
    requisition of, 79-80
    responsibilities of, 81
    acquisition of, 82-4
Prudence, 38
Punishment, 18
   ,,   capital, 132-138
Purity, 74

R

REASON, 11
Recreation, 95-7
Relativism, 8, 10-11, 14
Responsibility, 19
Retribution, 18

INDEX

Revelation, need of, 14-6
Right and wrong, definition of, 8
    ,,   ,,   distinction between, 10
Rights, human :
    respect for, 72-4
  ,, family, 74
  ,, violation of, 136-7

S

SANDERSON, ROBERT, 57-8
Self-deception, 15
Selfishness, human, 14
Sex, 104-122
Sin, 30-1, 36
  ,, violation of conscience, 36-7
Sins, capital, 39
Sloth, 40
Society :
    Man's need of, 12
    Definition of, 60
Speech, functions of, 105
Suicide, 123-4
Surrender, 43

T

TAYLOR, JEREMY, 63
Taxes, 67-8
Temperance, 38
Theodorit, 63

U

UTILITARIANISM, 8-9

V

VIRTUES, 11
    cardinal, 38
    faith, 37-8
    humility, 18
    justice, 12, 38
    theological, 38

W

WAR, 24, 27
  ,, civil, 57
  ,, justification of, 127-8
Women, status of, 20